Y0-CUZ-201

947
SYM
  Symynkywicz, Jeffrey
    The Soviet turmoil

C1

DATE DUE			

GALILEO S.A. LIBRARY
820 S. CARPENTER ST.
CHICAGO, IL 60607

THE FALL OF COMMUNISM

by Jeffrey B. Symynkywicz

GALILEO S.A. LIBRARY
820 S. CARPENTER ST.
CHICAGO, IL 60607

Dillon Press • Parsippany, New Jersey

For Noah, who fills us with surprise, wonder, and joy

Photo Credits
Front Cover: Pascal Le Segretain/Sygma Photo News.

AP/Wide World Photos: 65, 72, 86, 102, 123. Corbis-Bettmann News Photos: 10, 22, 38, 67; Reuters: 71, 94, 99, 106; UPI: 6, 29, 48. Culver Pictures: 8. Liaison International: 41; Chip Hires: 144; Georges Merllon: 135; Vlastimir Shone: 80; URSS: 131. Sygma Photo News/Henry Bureau: 45. Sovfoto: 13, 20; Eastfoto: 54, 60, 89 l.; Itar-Tass: 89 r., 141.

Library of Congress Cataloging-in-Publication Data
Symynkywicz, Jeffrey.
  The Soviet turmoil / Jeffrey B. Symynkywicz.
    p. cm. — (Fall of communism)
  Includes bibliographical references and index.
  Summary: Studies the people, events, and other factors that played a role in the founding, development, and collapse of the Soviet Union.
  ISBN 0-87518-633-5 (LSB). — ISBN 0-382-39301-5 (pbk.)
  1. Soviet Union—History—Juvenile literature. [1. Soviet Union—History.] I. Title. II. Series.
DK266.S98 1997
947—dc20   95-35511

Copyright © 1997 by Jeffrey Symynkywicz
All rights reserved. No part of this book may be reproduced or transmitted in any form or by any means, electronic or mechanical, including photocopying, recording, or by any information storage and retrieval system, without permission in writing from the Publisher.

Published by Dillon Press,
A Division of Simon & Schuster,
299 Jefferson Road, Parsippany, NJ 07054

First edition

Printed in the United States of America

10 9 8 7 6 5 4 3 2 1

CONTENTS

- Chapter 1   "A Worker's Paradise"   7
- Chapter 2   The Stalin Terror   19
- Chapter 3   Khrushchev and De-Stalinization   33
- Chapter 4   Eras of Stagnation   44
- Chapter 5   Gorbachev: Like a Breath of Fresh Air   58
- Chapter 6   Hard-liners vs. Reformers   69
- Chapter 7   Winters of Discontent   82
- Chapter 8   Out of Control   97
- Chapter 9   The Coup   115
- Chapter 10   New Flag over the Kremlin   132
- Chapter Notes   146
- Glossary   150
- Time Line   152
- Selected Bibliography   155
- Index   158

Czar Nicholas II addressing some troops on the eastern front

chapter 1

"A Worker's Paradise"

There were two revolutions in Russia in 1917—the March Revolution and the November Revolution (or, according to the old-style calendar in use in Russia until 1918, the February Revolution and the October Revolution).* Both broke out in the Russian capital, Petrograd, and would have long-lasting effects far beyond Russia.

Since 1914, Russia had been entangled in the Great War (World War I). Casualties were enormous. More than 1,600,000 Russians would be killed by war's end. The Russian economy could not hold up under the weight of the conflict. Neither the needs of the troops at the front nor those of the people back home could be met. By 1916, with his army facing defeat at the hands of German forces, Czar Nicholas II assumed control of Russia's war effort. His wife, the Czarina Alexandra, took control of domestic affairs. She was greatly influenced by her chief advisor, a mysterious Siberian peasant named Grigori Rasputin, who had gained a reputation as a holy man.

Support for the czar quickly vanished. Not even the assassination of the "mad monk" Rasputin late in 1916 could save the Romanov dynasty, which had held power

---

*All dates in this book are based on the new calendar, which is used today.

8   The Soviet Turmoil

Czar Nicholas II and his family

for 300 years. As the winter of 1917 dragged on, the nation became more exhausted. Then on March 8, Petrograd's bread supply ran out, and hungry workers took to the streets. Armed troops were sent in to put down the protests, but some soon joined the striking workers instead. Nicholas's position swiftly deteriorated. Members of the State Duma—the legislative body established in 1905 to advise the czar—soon were calling upon him to abdicate, to give up his throne to save the war effort. On March 15, Nicholas II finally handed over power to the State Duma. A provisional government under Prince Georgi Lvov was to hold power until a freely elected Constituent Assembly drew up a permanent constitution. Soviets, or councils, were formed in cities across Russia to protect the interests of the working class.

Conflict soon arose between the soviets and the provisional

government, however. In its first official act, the Petrograd Soviet decreed that all units of the Russian army were to be governed by elected committees. As a result the Russian army was soon in a complete shambles, allowing German forces to move steadily eastward.

This system of "dual authority," with the provisional government and the soviets vying for control, greatly weakened Russia. It was in these uneasy times that the Communist leader Vladimir Ilyich Lenin returned to his homeland.

Lenin had been arrested in 1895 for his revolutionary activities and exiled to Siberia in 1897, after being held for questioning for over a year. Three years later he got permission to leave Russia and went to Germany. There he founded the newspaper *Iskra* (which means "Spark") as the official journal of the Russian Social Democratic Labor Party (RSDLP). Not all Russian followers of the German political thinker Karl Marx agreed with the ideas Lenin championed in *Iskra*, especially his belief that only a relatively small, tightly disciplined party of professional revolutionaries could lead the movement to victory. Others believed that the RSDLP should become instead a mass party seeking power through democratic means. Soon the party was openly split, and by the time of the 1903 party conference, the more zealous faction headed by Lenin held a slight majority. They took the name Bolsheviks (after the Russian word for "majority"). Their more democratic-oriented rivals accepted the name Mensheviks (or "minority").

Lenin was living in Switzerland when the March Revolution broke out. When the czar was finally toppled,

Lenin made his way back to Russia with the help of the German military command. The Germans hoped that Lenin would use his influence to end his country's involvement in the war. In April 1917, Lenin boarded a train in Zurich and was given free passage across German territory into Russia.

Lenin received a hero's welcome on his return to Russia on April 16. Even members of the provisional government were on hand to greet him as his train arrived at Petrograd's Finland Station. But unlike most of the revolutionaries already in Russia, Lenin would not bow to the new authorities. In a series of speeches later known as the April Theses, Lenin declared that it was time to begin the next stage of Russia's historical development—the building of socialism.

Lenin's proposed program was radical and direct: Russia must immediately withdraw from the war with Germany. Local soviets should assume control of the government.

Lenin speaking before the troops in Red Square, Moscow

Land should be confiscated and redistributed among the peasants, and workers should be given control of the factories in which they labored.

Lenin's refusal to compromise struck a responsive chord among many Russians who were losing patience with the provisional government. Support for the Bolsheviks rose steadily, and Lenin waited for an opportunity for his party to seize power. Many believed such an opportunity was at hand in July 1917. For two days, rebellious soldiers rampaged through the streets of Petrograd, firing their rifles into the air and demanding that the provisional government step down. Soon they were joined by thousands of radical workers, and then by more than 5,000 mutinous sailors stationed on Kronstadt, an island in the Baltic.

Lenin, however, feared that the explosive popular uprising may have come too soon. But he and the rest of the Bolshevik leadership saw no choice but to lend their support, somewhat reluctantly, to the violent protests of the "July Days." When the Petrograd soviet withheld its support for the insurrection and when most units of the Russian army remained loyal to the provisional government, the rebellion was doomed. The government quickly moved additional troops into the capital, and peace was soon restored to the streets of Petrograd.

Many people blamed the Bolsheviks for the rebellion. Arrest warrants were issued for Lenin and other party leaders. "Now they will shoot us down, one by one," Lenin predicted. "This is the right time for them."[1] He quickly made plans to escape across the border into Finland. But the defeat of the July Days rebellion proved only a temporary setback to the Communist movement. Although the provisional government, now under the leadership of Aleksandr Kerensky, attempted to deal more forcibly with its enemies, Russia still faced enormous problems. Kerensky promised to take action to improve the lives of the country's poorer citizens but received little popular support. The more radical members of Russian society were critical of Kerensky's moderation, while conservative forces, including many of the commanders of the Russian army, were distrustful of Kerensky's socialist tendencies.

Late in August, General Lavr Kornilov, commander in chief of the Russian armed forces, moved his troops north toward Petrograd in an attempt to seize power. Alarmed, Kerensky released all imprisoned Bolshevik leaders and armed the members of the Bolshevik militia so that they could join in the anticipated fight against Kornilov. But when Kornilov's rebellion bogged down far south of Petrograd, Kerensky's bold move backfired, and the Bolsheviks found themselves free, armed—and stronger than ever.

As time went on, Kerensky and the moderates seemed to grow steadily weaker in the face of the crisis Russia faced. Rather than taking bold, decisive action to deal with Russia's problems, Kerensky organized a series of large conferences to *discuss* the issues. In contrast the slogans offered by Lenin and the Bolsheviks—"Bread, peace, and land" and "All Power to the Soviets"—seemed strikingly simple and direct and ultimately had broader appeal. The Bolsheviks gained a majority in the Petrograd soviet, and one of the party's leaders, Leon Trotsky, was chosen council chairman. Several days later the Bolsheviks also gained control of the soviet in Moscow.

"History will not forgive us if we do not assume power now," Lenin wrote at this time.[2] But other Bolshevik leaders still argued for a more gradual approach. After a long debate the central committee of the party supported Lenin. However, over his objections it also decided to

Soldiers and armed civilians *(foreground)* gather in front of the Winter Palace.

delay the armed uprising until the scheduled meeting of the national Congress of Soviets in Petrograd in early November. At the Congress, a nonviolent seizure of power would be attempted. Only if that failed would the Bolsheviks resort to arms.

But the provisional government forced the party's hand. On November 6, just as the Congress of Soviets prepared to convene, Kerensky declared a state of emergency. Troops loyal to the government occupied important positions around the capital. The next day, Kerensky outlawed the Bolshevik party. Trotsky then appealed to the army—now heavily infiltrated by Communists—to come to the assistance of the beleaguered Petrograd soviet. Thousands of prosoviet troops stormed into the capital. The forces of the provisional government were badly outnumbered, and they surrendered quickly.

The next night, November 7, soldiers loyal to the Bolsheviks seized control of the Winter Palace, the seat of the Russian government. Following a week of fierce fighting, Moscow also came under Bolshevik control. The second revolution of 1917, the November Revolution (also called the Great October Socialist Revolution, following the old calendar), had established the world's first Communist state.

▼ ▲ ▼

On November 8, 1917, the All-Russian Congress of Soviets met in Petrograd. Lenin was chosen as chair of Russia's new government, the Council of People's Commissars. He moved quickly to fulfill the promises that the Bolsheviks had made prior to taking power. Large landholdings were confiscated and divided among the peasants. Factories were taken over by the government and were to be run by committees of workers. Lenin also announced an immediate cessation of hostilities in the war with Germany.

Germany, however, quickly rejected the Bolsheviks' offer of a peace "without annexations or indemnities," that is, a peace that restored the boundaries that had existed before the Great War began. The German high command realized that Russia no longer had either the ability or the will to continue the fight. In February 1918 the kaiser's army began moving east toward Moscow, where the Bolsheviks had moved the national capital.

A Bolshevik delegation hurried to the front lines to sue for peace. On March 3 the Treaty of Brest-Litovsk was signed. Russia was allowed to withdraw from the war, but lost control of Lithuania, Latvia, Estonia, Finland, Poland, the Ukraine, and much of Byelorussia—nearly 1 million square kilometers of territory and home to more than 60 million people. Even Lenin characterized the terms of the Treaty of Brest-Litovsk as "shameful."[3]

The war with Germany was over, but the battle for the existence of the Soviet state was far from complete. The Red Army was formed and placed under the command of Trotsky. Soon the Bolsheviks' enemies within Russia formed an army of their own (generally referred to as the White Army). The group was a wide-ranging, loosely organized coalition of democrats, czarists, cossacks, Social Revolutionaries, Mensheviks, and anarchists, who were united only in their common hatred of the Bolsheviks.

From 1918 to 1920, Russia was torn by civil war. It was a time of misery for the entire country. At the same time, Russia's former allies in the Great War attempted to bring down the Communist state. A blockade was imposed, and French, British, and American troops invaded Russia in support of the White Army's cause. But the domestic enemies of Bolshevik power proved disunited and weak, and their foreign allies were too exhausted from the rigors of the Great War to mount another great fight in Russia. The new Communist state survived.

Lenin had hoped that the Bolshevik victory would lead to a series of workers' revolutions throughout Europe. But the long-anticipated uprising of the working class, or proletariat, never came. Nevertheless, the establishment of Soviet Russia was greeted eagerly and hopefully by many people, who believed that Russia's new "state of workers and peasants" would provide the world with a new model for social justice and economic equity. Soon, however, the inherently undemocratic nature of the Communist state became apparent.

Lenin looked upon the institutions of parliamentary democracy with disdain. Just after the November

Revolution, the Bolsheviks grudgingly allowed already scheduled open elections for a new national Constituent Assembly to proceed as planned. The clear victors in the election were the Bolsheviks' chief rivals, the Socialist Revolutionaries, who gained an absolute majority, 370 of 707 seats. The Bolsheviks held only 170. Clearly, Lenin would not be able to rely on the Constituent Assembly to carry out his will.

As the delegates gathered on January 5, Lenin said to a friend, "Since we made the mistake of promising the world that this talk shop would meet, we have to open it up today, but history has not yet said a word about when we will shut it down."[4] The very next morning, Lenin and the Council of People's Commissars declared the National Assembly dissolved and ordered troops to disperse the gathered delegates. There would be no sharing of power as long as the Bolsheviks were in control of the government.

Lenin also endorsed the use of terror in building the new Communist state. In December 1917 the Extraordinary Commission to Combat Counterrevolution, known by its Russian acronym Cheka, was established. Felix Dzerzhinsky was named its first director. The Cheka was the revolution's secret police. It directed the suppression of the Communists' internal enemies. Among the Red Terror's earliest victims had been the former czar, Nicholas II, and his family. The czar; his wife, Alexandra; and their five children were shot by a Soviet firing squad at Yekaterinburg on July 17, 1918.

Also in July 1918 the Bolsheviks' former allies, the Left Socialist Revolutionaries, or the Left SRs, made a feeble attempt to seize control. The attempted coup was quickly put down, but a little more than a month later a Left SR agent assassinated the chief of the Petrograd Cheka,

Mikhail Uritsky. That same day, another Left SR, Dora Kaplan, shot and wounded Lenin at a workers' meeting in Moscow. The Communist central committee then ordered the Cheka to carry out "merciless mass terror" against the enemies of the regime across the country.

In Petrograd alone, more than 500 "class enemies" were executed. Elsewhere, tens of thousands of "people of high social position, large landowners, factory owners, prominent officials and academics, close relatives of people formerly in power,"[5] and others were arrested by the Cheka and incarcerated in special prisons known as concentration camps (a term coined by Trotsky). During the first half of 1918, the Cheka had executed only 22 "class enemies" in the name of the revolution. During the second half of the year, more than 6,000 were shot and tens of thousands of others arrested.

Soviet Communism soon faced an even greater crisis. In May 1922, Lenin suffered a stroke. For more than five months, he lay completely incapacitated. In early October he was able to resume some of his duties, but two months later another stroke took an even greater toll. Even after recovering from this stroke, Lenin could work only a short while each day. From his bed he would dictate a few thoughts to his secretary, who would scrupulously copy each word the great revolutionary said.

Between December 24 and December 26, 1922, Lenin dictated a letter to the Twelfth Party Congress that was scheduled to meet in the spring. This document is commonly referred to as Lenin's Testament. More than anything, perhaps, the ailing leader feared a divisive struggle for power within the party after he died. Both of the men most often mentioned as possible successors, Josef Stalin and Leon Trotsky, presented problems for Lenin.

> *Comrade Stalin, on becoming General Secretary, concentrated enormous power in his hands, and I am not always sure he always knows how to use this power carefully enough. On the other hand, Comrade Trotsky is distinguished not only by outstanding abilities. . . . Personally, he is, I daresay, the most capable member of the present Central Committee, but he is possessed by excessive self-confidence and by excessive infatuation for the purely administrative side of things.*[6]

Nine days later, Lenin added a postscript to his Testament, which contained an even more stinging denunciation of Stalin.

> *Stalin is too coarse, and this fault, though quite tolerable in relations among us Communists becomes intolerable in the office of General Secretary. Therefore I suggest to the comrades that they think of a way of transferring Stalin from this position and assigning another man to it who differs from Comrade Stalin only in one superiority: more tolerant, more loyal, more polite, and more considerate of his comrades. . . .*[7]

Perhaps Lenin hoped that the central committee would rely upon a collective leadership, rather than a single leader, after his death. But when Lenin's death—from a massive cerebral hemorrhage—finally came on January 21, 1924, the question of who would succeed him as head of the Soviet Communist Party was still unresolved.

chapter 2

The Stalin Terror

Stalin moved quickly to fashion himself as Lenin's legitimate heir. Just five days after the great Bolshevik's death, Stalin delivered the oration at Lenin's memorial service. Sounding more like a Russian Orthodox priest than an atheistic Communist leader, Stalin praised the fallen leader with an almost religious reverence.

> *Departing from us, Comrade Lenin adjured us to hold high and guard the purity of the great title of member of the party. We vow to you, Comrade Lenin, that we will fulfill your behest with honor!*
>
> *Departing from us, Comrade Lenin adjured us to guard the unity of our party as the apple of our eye. We vow to you, Comrade Lenin, that this behest, too, we will fulfill with honor!*
>
> *Departing from us, Comrade Lenin adjured us to strengthen the dictatorship of the proletariat. We vow to you, Comrade Lenin, that we will spare no effort to fulfill this behest, too, with honor! . . .*[1]

As party secretary, Stalin had the responsibility of overseeing the details of Lenin's funeral. Trotsky was conspicuously absent and later claimed Stalin had given him the wrong date! In addition, Stalin authorized the

Stalin (*left front*) is among those carrying the casket of Lenin to a tomb in Red Square.

embalming of Lenin's body and the construction of an ornate tomb in Red Square in Moscow, in which the body was to lie permanently. Finally, in 1925, Petrograd, the nation's second largest city, was renamed Leningrad.

Stalin also moved quickly to outmaneuver any possible rivals. In January 1925, Trotsky was removed as commissar for war. Stalin then turned vehemently against his former allies, Grigori Zinoviev and Lev Kamenev. By the end of the year, Zinoviev had lost his position as head of the Leningrad party branch, and Kamenev was replaced as party leader for Moscow. When the pair lamely attempted to join with Trotsky in a united opposition, Stalin moved ruthlessly to crush them. At the Fifteenth Party Congress in December 1927, the members of the opposition were expelled from the Communist Party, and all "deviation from the general party line" (as interpreted by Stalin) was staunchly condemned.

Having dealt with the "Left Opposition" of Trotsky, Zinoviev, and Kamenev, Stalin turned against "Rightists" within the party. This group, which favored the continuation of the policies of the NEP and a more gradual building of socialism, was led by Nikolai Bukharin. Bukharin was a brilliant young Communist who served as editor of the party newspaper, *Pravda*. In April 1929 Bukharin was fired from this position. Seven months later he was expelled from the Politburo, or executive committee of the party, as well.

By his fiftieth birthday in December 1929, Stalin held dictatorial power over the Soviet party and state. Grand festivities celebrating the "great teacher" Stalin were held in cities across the land. Articles in the government press lauded him as "remarkable," "a genius," Lenin's one true disciple.

Stalin laid the foundation of the Soviet state—or Union of Soviet Socialist Republics as it was renamed in 1922—which would survive for the next 60 years. The First Five-Year Plan, begun in 1929, changed the face of the Soviet economy. Over 1,500 new factories were constructed, including huge industrial complexes like Magnitostroi and Kuznetstroi. Magnitogorsk, an entirely new industrial city in the central Urals, would have a population of over 250,000 by 1932.

Implementation of the plan in agriculture proved more troublesome. Even though Communism was supposedly based on the interests of the industrial working class, Russia remained largely an agricultural society. The vast majority of its people were impoverished, illiterate peasants who continued to live life in much the same manner as

22　The Soviet Turmoil

their prerevolutionary forebears. Stalin decided that only through full-scale collectivization, or forced government takeover of the nation's farmland, would agricultural production be able to meet the needs of the USSR's rapidly expanding labor force.

No one in the countryside would be allowed to resist Stalin's decision. Hundreds of thousands of dedicated, specially trained party officials, known as cadres, were sent into villages across the land. These cadres were often accompanied by agents of the secret police, who also helped to convince the peasants to accept collectivization peacefully. If the peasants in a particular village resisted, however, units of the Soviet Red Army were mobilized to bring matters under control.

Peasant resistance was especially strong in the fertile

Stalin is shown here during a visit to a collective farm.

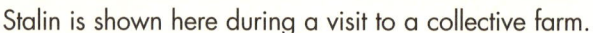

western plains of the Ukraine. An eyewitness of one rebellion in the eastern Ukraine gives a horrifying account.

In 1930, in the Dnieperpropetrovsk region thousands of peasants armed with hunting rifles, axes, and pitchforks revolted against the regime. . . . NKVD [secret police] units and militia were sent. For three days . . . a bloody battle was waged between the revolting people and the authorities. . . . This revolt was cruelly punished. Thousands . . . paid for the attempt with their lives, while the survivors were deported to concentration camps. In the villages of Ternovka and Boganovka . . . mass executions were carried out near the balkis [ravines]. The soil of the region was soaked in blood. After the executions, these villages were set on fire. [2]

Stalin also attempted to turn poor peasants against their wealthier neighbors, the kulaks. In 1929 the central committee decreed "the liquidation of the kulaks as a class" and enlisted the assistance of the poorer peasants in their campaigns of "dekulakization."

Government agents encouraged poor peasants to attack the kulaks, to loot and burn their houses, and to terrorize them and drive them from the area. By 1933 over 1 million kulak families—in all, about 5 million men, women, and children—were deported to concentration camps in eastern Siberia or to the frozen Arctic north. Thousands never reached their destination.

Trainloads of deported peasants left for the icy North, the forests, the steppes, the deserts. There were whole populations, denuded of everything; the old folk starved to death in mid-journey,

> *newborn babies were buried on the banks of the roadside, and each wilderness had its crop of little crosses of boughs of white wood.*[3]

The costs of collectivization were horrendous. Hundreds of thousands of peasants slaughtered their livestock rather than allow it to be taken by the state. Between 1929 and 1933 the number of cattle, horses, sheep, goats, and hogs in the Soviet Union declined by about 50 percent.

The problems of collectivization, combined with poor weather, made the 1932 harvest one of the worst on record. Nevertheless, the government demanded the full quota needed to fulfill the plan. Often nothing was left to feed the people of the villages once the government had carted away its share. People were forced to eat anything they could get their hands on—cats, dogs, mice, the bark from trees, even horse manure. There were even reports of cannibalism. In some villages, every child under the age of three died from the effects of the famine. During the winter of 1932–33, at least 5 million Soviet peasants starved to death.

Yet Stalin pushed forward relentlessly with the plan. By the Seventeenth Party Congress in January 1934, he declared that, with the completion of the First Five-Year Plan, there was "nothing more to prove and . . . no one left to fight."[4] Some Soviet citizens dared to hope that the most severe rigors of industrialization and collectivization were over, but they were soon to discover that their terror had only begun.

On December 1, 1934, the first secretary of the Leningrad Communist Party, Sergei Kirov, was assassinated. Whether, as many historians believe, Stalin ordered Kirov's death or not, he nonetheless seized upon the murder with a vengeance. The Soviet press declared that the murder of Kirov, who had been widely mentioned as Stalin's possible successor, was proof that agents from the capitalist West were trying to undermine the world's first workers' state. The very existence of socialism was at stake, Stalin declared.

Throughout the country, hundreds of thousands of people were arrested and deported to the concentration camps of Siberia. New laws were passed allowing children as young as 12 to be executed for sabotage against the state. Stalin's main rivals—Zinoviev, Kamenev, and Bukharin (Trotsky had been deported in 1929)—were promptly arrested.

Between 1936 and 1938 the Soviet government staged great "show trials" of the leading "enemies of the people." Prosecuting the case for the state, Andrei Vyshinsky declared that the defendants had led a conspiracy of "Rightists, Trotskyists, Mensheviks, Socialist Revolutionaries, bourgeois nationalists, and so on and so forth." They were, he said, a "foul-smelling heap of human garbage," who represented "the scum and filth of the past." They were, Vyshinsky concluded, "hateful traitors" who "must be shot like mad dogs."[5]

No evidence was ever offered of the heinous crimes purportedly committed by the defendants. All, however, gave long, demeaning confessions as they stood before the bar. These confessions were motivated by a number of factors: a desire to save their families future hardship; a belief that, somehow, by confessing they helped to ensure the building of communism; and—not the least—the painful memory of long, brutal hours of torture at the hands of the secret police.

Of the leading defendants at the first three show trials, all

54 were found guilty. Fifty of these were summarily executed; four disappeared into the camps. They were not alone. Stalin's terror eventually claimed close to 60 percent of the delegates to the 1934 Communist Party "Congress of Victors." Seventy percent of the Congress's central committee was wiped out. In the party's lower ranks, the effects of the purge were even more devastating.

Stalin then turned on the Soviet military. In 1935, Stalin had created the new post of marshal of the Soviet Union, to which he had named five of the Red Army's leading generals. By 1938, three of the generals had been executed. Of the 16 chief army commanders, 15 were killed in the purges. Likewise, all 4 fleet admirals and 15 of 21 admirals of the Soviet navy were executed.

The Great Terror devoured even its own perpetrators. Genrikh Yagdoa, chief of the secret police at the outset of the purges, was shot along with Bukharin in 1938. He was succeeded by Nikolai Yezhov, who would lead the Great Terror during the time of its greatest intensity. Indeed, this period in Soviet history is sometimes referred to as the *Yezhovchina* because of the role played by Yezhov. When Yezhov was executed in 1938 and replaced by Lavrenti Beria, some saw it as a sign that the worst of the Great Terror was over.

In spite of the extent of the Stalinist famine and terror, the prestige of the USSR rose steadily abroad. Although most of the nations of the world had extended diplomatic recognition to the Soviet government by 1935, Stalin still feared the formation of a great capitalist alliance against him. When Hitler came to power in Germany in 1933,

Stalin suspected that a new French-German alliance might free the Nazi leader to attack the Soviet Union. Thus Stalin decided that he would beat the French to the punch and enter into his own agreement with Nazi Germany.

Long, difficult negotiations took place between the Soviet foreign minister, V. M. Molotov, and his German counterpart, Joachim von Ribbentrop. Finally, on August 23, 1939, a German-Soviet nonaggression pact was signed. Publicly the agreement simply established diplomatic relations between the two countries and committed each side not to attack the other. But secret side agreements went even further. Poland was to be partitioned between Germany and the USSR. The USSR agreed not to interfere in Germany's designs on the Bessarabian oil fields in Romania, and, for its part, Germany agreed not to interfere should the Soviet Union seek to extend its influence over the Romanian region of Moldavia and the Baltic republics Lithuania, Latvia, and Estonia.

One week later, on September 1, 1939, Germany invaded Poland. Soviet troops then moved in and annexed the eastern part of that country. Great Britain and France came to Poland's aid, and World War II began.

Stalin was able to avoid involvement in the Second World War for almost two years. But at four o'clock in the morning on June 22, 1941, Germany and its allies launched an attack along the entire length of the German-Soviet border. The German air force, the Luftwaffe, bombed major airfields in the eastern USSR. By the end of the day, German troops had advanced almost 50 miles into Soviet territory.

Stalin seemed paralyzed at first, unable to act. He could not believe that the Germans had violated their agreement with him. Then, on July 3—11 days after the invasion and with foreign troops already hundreds of miles into Soviet territory—Stalin addressed the people of the USSR.

> *Comrades! Citizens! Brothers and sisters! Men of our army and navy! I am addressing you, my friends.*
>
> *The perfidious military attack on our fatherland, begun on June 22 by Hitler's Germany, is continuing.*
>
> *In spite of the heroic resistance of the Red Army, and although the enemy's finest divisions and air force units have already been smashed and have met their doom on the field of battle, the enemy continues to push forward, hurling fresh forces into the attack....*
>
> *A grave danger hangs over our country.*[6]

Indeed, the very existence of the Soviet Union was at stake. Through tactics of *Blitzkrieg* ("lightning war"), Hitler hoped to take Moscow by the end of the summer, certainly before winter came. Although fierce fighting at Smolensk, near the center of the front, slowed the German advance, in October German tanks were able to breach the Soviet lines at Mozhaisk, just 65 miles from the Soviet capital. Fearing that a German attack on Moscow was imminent, Stalin and the Soviet leadership fled over 500 miles southeast to Kuibyshev. The invading troops advanced to within 25 miles of Moscow before being stopped by Red Army forces under the command of Marshal Georgi Zhukov.

But German hopes for a quick victory faded as the long Russian winter set in. The tide of the war turned. The German army laid siege to Leningrad, but the city held out

The Stalin Terror   29

Surrounded by Russian soldiers, German troops come out of a house in the Kharkov area.

for almost 900 days. In early 1942 the Red Army began to recapture areas on the southern front.

Hitler struggled to keep the fight going. His chief general advised an orderly retreat from Russian territory, but he refused to consider such a plan. A final German offensive in July 1943 was turned back by the Red Army, and by mid-1944 the Soviets had driven the Germans from the territory of the USSR and into Poland. The long pursuit of the Germans to Berlin had begun.

On D-day—June 6, 1944—the Allies stormed the beaches of Normandy, France, and the second front for which Stalin had been lobbying since 1942 finally was opened. Later, Stalin and the Soviet leadership would insist that they, in fact, had been the critical factor in the defeat of Hitler. For two years prior to D-day, the Red Army had borne the brunt of Hitler's fury alone and eventually had prevailed. The cost had been very high. By the time of Germany's surrender in May 1945, the Second World War had cost the lives of perhaps 20 million Soviet citizens.

▼ ▲ ▼

Though his country was in a shambles, Stalin emerged from the war stronger than ever. Through skillful diplomacy and political maneuvering, the Soviets managed to gain control of an extensive sphere of influence in central and eastern Europe. One by one, Communist "people's democracies" were established in Albania, Bulgaria, Czechoslovakia, East Germany, Hungary, Poland, Romania, and Yugoslavia. When the iron curtain of the cold war fell between East and West, Stalin stood securely as the acknowledged leader of one of the world's two great power blocs.

But not even victory could ease Stalin's fear and paranoia. The Soviet people must not let down their guard, he said. Soviet soldiers who had spent years in enemy prisoner-of-war camps were arrested as soon as they reached Soviet territory. Those who had "allowed" themselves to be captured were automatically classified as cowards and traitors. Thousands were either shot or sent to labor camps.

Stalin also feared the influence of "decadent" Western

ideas in the Soviet Union. Leading Soviet writers, composers, and artists were criticized for their "antisocialist" ideas. Jazz and other Western artistic forms were banned. Everything Russian was praised; everything foreign was suspect.

Stalin had other targets, too. He singled out the Jews of the Soviet Union as a special target of hate. Early in 1948 the Soviet authorities claimed that there was a conspiracy on the part of Soviet Jews to establish a foothold for American imperialism in Soviet territory. Immediately hundreds of leaders of the Jewish community were executed or arrested by the secret police.

Stalin's antisemitic mania seemed to know no bounds. In January 1953 several leading physicians at the Kremlin hospital—all of them Jewish—supposedly confessed to conspiring to kill a wide array of Soviet leaders, including Stalin himself. The Communist party organized mass meetings across the country to denounce the "doctor-murderers." Soon, ordinary Soviet citizens began to refuse treatment from Jewish doctors. Jews were summarily beaten as they walked down the streets of their cities. Government institutions began compiling lists of Jewish employees in preparation for future disciplinary action. The loyalty and trustworthiness of all Soviet Jews was called into question. Many people believed that Stalin was preparing to unleash another large-scale terror campaign, this time aimed specifically against the Jewish population. Some even believed that Stalin intended to banish all Soviet Jews to the easternmost reaches of Siberia.

But Stalin did not live to carry out his plans. In February 1953, he suffered a stroke. Shortly thereafter, on March 5, the Soviet dictator died. The "Doctors' Plot" and the anti-Jewish campaign quietly receded from the national consciousness.

Immediately the Soviet party became involved in an intense struggle for power. Leading members of the Politburo even argued among themselves over who should stand vigil by the casket of the dead leader! There were other arguments as well about who should be in charge of the arrangements for Stalin's funeral, who should deliver the eulogy, and how long each member of the Politburo should be allowed to speak.

On the day of the funeral, millions of Soviet citizens crowded the streets of Moscow, all making their way to the government palace where the dead dictator lay in state. Eventually the crowds grew so large and the procession became so closely packed together that perhaps as many as 500 mourners were crushed or trampled to death. The tragedy marked a horrible end to a horrendous political career. Even in death, it seemed, the man who had terrorized the Soviet Union for almost 30 years, whose policies had caused the death of at least 20 to 30 million people, continued to claim the lives of his nation's citizens.

chapter 3

Khrushchev and De-Stalinization

The people of the USSR—indeed, much of the world—waited expectantly as the men at the top of the Soviet Communist hierarchy jostled for position to succeed Stalin. At first, Georgi Malenkov, second secretary in the Politburo after Stalin, seemed the most powerful member of the new "collective leadership." Immediately following Stalin's death, Malenkov was named Soviet prime minister, or premier, as well as first secretary of the Communist Party. One rung down from Malenkov was Lavrenti Beria, Stalin's security chief, who was to remain in control of the interior ministry and the secret police. Widely seen as third in importance was V. M. Molotov, the foreign minister.

Within two weeks, however, the makeup of the Soviet leadership changed yet again. On March 14, Malenkov asked to be relieved of his position as first secretary of the party so that he might concentrate on running the government. He was replaced as party leader by Nikita Khrushchev, whom most observers believed ranked behind Malenkov, Beria, and Molotov in power and influence.

But soon Khrushchev joined with Malenkov and Molotov against their common enemy—Beria. At a meeting of the party's ruling circle in the summer of 1953, Beria was arrested. Later he was accused of having been a spy for Great Britain for more than 20 years—an accusation with no basis in fact. Within a few months, Beria and his "accomplices" in the interior ministry supposedly were tried, found guilty, and sentenced to death. In actual fact, however, Beria had been executed shortly after his arrest.

Next to fall was Malenkov. Soon after coming to power, the new prime minister began to act on his promise to improve the living conditions of the Soviet people. Malenkov decreed that in the future the Soviet economy would put less emphasis on the development of heavy industry and more on the production of better-quality consumer goods.

Many common Soviet citizens were encouraged by their government's new policies. The powerful managers of the country's large industrial concerns, however, were not. Malenkov also alienated the high command of the Soviet armed forces when he proposed cutting spending on the military. As the chief administrator within the party, Khrushchev learned quickly of the discontent of high party members across the USSR. He gradually appointed his own supporters to leadership positions within the party. By the end of 1954, people loyal to Khrushchev, rather than to Malenkov, were in control of the party organization in the two largest Soviet cities, Moscow and Leningrad, as well as in more than half of the country's provinces.

Khrushchev was now able to make his move against Malenkov. At a meeting of the party's central committee in January 1955, the premier's policies were openly criticized. One month later Malenkov resigned. The new Soviet prime minister was Nikolai Bulganin, a close supporter of Khrushchev.

Nikita Khrushchev was now the most powerful man in the Soviet Union. But almost from the outset, the wily leader from the Ukraine seemed interested in more than personal power alone. Hoping to transform the USSR into a model for emerging nations, Khrushchev traveled extensively, showering friendly countries with vast amounts of technical and monetary assistance. Through the "Virgin Lands" campaign, he sought to put vast areas of previously uncultivated land into production, thus creating a dramatic and rapid increase in agricultural output. Khrushchev also allowed a moderate amount of free artistic expression in Soviet literature and the arts—the first such liberalization since the 1920s.

▼ ▲ ▼

But Khrushchev also realized that unless Soviet society was cleansed of all remaining vestiges of the Stalinist era, his plans to transform the USSR into a thoroughly modern socialist state would come to nothing. By 1956, Khrushchev had come to believe that a dramatic break with the past was needed.

Late on the night of February 24, 1956, Khrushchev called an unscheduled, private session of the central committee of the Communist Party, which was in the midst of its Twentieth Party Congress. The tired delegates reluctantly made their way to the Kremlin's Palace of the Congresses, wondering what business could possibly be transacted at such a late hour.

Khrushchev told the assembled delegates that he had called them together to report on the findings of a special commission that had been established to study abuses of power alleged to have been committed during the time of

Stalin. "It is impermissible and foreign to the spirit of Marxism-Leninism to elevate one person, to transform him into a superman possessing supernatural characteristics akin to those of a god," Khrushchev began. "Such a belief about a man, and specifically about Stalin, was cultivated among us for many years,"[1] he went on. Khrushchev emphasized that there had already been enough written concerning Stalin's merits and that it was now time to look at the negative effects that the cult of Stalin had had on the life of the Soviet Union. Then for more than three hours, Khrushchev detailed Stalin's crimes.

Stalin had plotted against Lenin in seizing power, Khrushchev said. He imposed his ideas upon others and did not work democratically with other party leaders. He completely overturned the Soviet legal system and used "extreme measures" and "mass repression"—arrest, imprisonment, terror, torture—to consolidate his own power. Stalin's foreign policy had left the Soviet Union unprepared for World War II, Khrushchev maintained, and Stalin's delay in mobilizing Soviet forces after the Germans had invaded had cost countless lives.

Then Khrushchev turned to a consideration of more recent years: "After the war . . . Stalin became even more capricious, irritable, and brutal; in particular his suspicion grew. His persecution mania reached unbelievable dimensions. Many workers were becoming enemies before his very eyes." The Doctors' Plot was a complete fabrication, Khrushchev declared, an utter lie cooked up by Stalin himself with the assistance of the evil Beria.

"Comrades," Khrushchev concluded, "we must abolish the cult of the individual decisively, once and for all. . . ."[2]

▼ ▲ ▼

Khrushchev had dared to speak the truth about Stalin. The effect of Khrushchev's condemnation of Stalin was especially dramatic in the satellite states of Eastern and Central Europe, which were linked politically to the Soviet Union.

On June 28, 1956, workers in the large state-owned automobile factory in the Polish city of Poznań went on strike to protest poor economic conditions. Soon, a large crowd of workers broke into the city police station and seized weapons. Soldiers who had been called out to disperse the workers decided instead to join the protest. The Communist government of Poland declared a state of emergency. Heavily armed troops and tanks were sent into Poznań, and 48 Polish workers were killed and hundreds injured before the strike was finally put down.

In Hungary a reform-minded Communist named Imre Nagy had become prime minister shortly after Stalin's death. Nagy soon announced a program called the New Course, which proposed democratic reforms, including a more independent approach in Hungary's relations with the Soviet Union.

Nagy faced stern opposition from hard-line Stalinists within his own country. But after Khrushchev's speech, support for Nagy among Hungary's people grew. On October 23, 1956, thousands of people gathered in Budapest to demand democratic reforms and the removal of Soviet troops from Hungarian territory. At first it seemed as though many of the protesters' demands would be granted. On October 27, Prime Minister Nagy announced the formation of a new cabinet, which included

A bust of Joseph Stalin sits in a Budapest street after it was pulled down from its pedestal during the Hungarian uprising.

several prominent non-Communists. The next day the Soviet government announced that it would begin immediately to withdraw its troops from Hungary.

But on October 31, Nagy received reports that the Soviet Union was preparing for a massive invasion of Hungary. Feeling betrayed, Nagy summoned the Soviet ambassador, Yuri Andropov, to his office and informed him that Hungary was withdrawing from the Warsaw Pact, the alliance of Soviet bloc nations, and would no longer be bound to the Soviet Union.

Andropov immediately informed his superiors in Moscow that Hungary's future as a socialist state was threatened. The next day the Soviet foreign ministry announced that Hungary was in the grips of an "antisocialist counterrevolution," and that Nagy himself was the leading traitor.

On November 4, thousands of Soviet troops stormed into Budapest, trampling all resistance. Within hours, Nagy and his government in the parliament buildings were surrounded—cut off from the outside world. By the time the Soviet takeover of the city was completed one week later, thousands had been killed and tens of thousands wounded. In the months that followed, over 20,000 Hungarians were sentenced to long prison terms, and more than 2,000 Freedom Fighters—including Nagy and members of his government—were executed for their role in the October uprising.

▼ ▲ ▼

In the Soviet Union, Khrushchev struggled to protect his reforms from the effects of the Hungarian uprising. Hard-line leaders within the party began to openly denounce Khrushchev's de-Stalinization program. Khrushchev, they said, was a "harebrained adventurist" whose ill-conceived policies might eventually topple the Soviet system. In May 1957 at a meeting of the presidium—the small, select ruling circle at the very top of the party hierarchy—the hard-liners almost managed to bring Khrushchev down.

But Khrushchev insisted on a vote of the entire central committee, which was his right under the terms of the party's constitution. Immediately, Khrushchev's close ally, Marshal Georgi Zhukov, the head of the Soviet defense ministry, commandeered military aircraft to fly

Khrushchev's supporters to Moscow for the special session. Ivan Serov, the head of the KGB, the state security police, used all means at his disposal to pressure wavering delegates to support Khrushchev.

When the entire central committee finally met to discuss Khrushchev's fate, an overwhelming majority reaffirmed their confidence in the first secretary. Moreover, the central committee also voted to strip all of Khrushchev's leading opponents of their posts. Their attempts to remove Khrushchev had backfired badly. Khrushchev was even named to replace Bulganin as premier.

By the time of the Twenty-second Congress of the party in October 1961, Khrushchev felt confident enough to step up the pace of de-Stalinization. All of the hundreds of cities, towns, factories, schools—even mountains and rivers—named after Stalin were to be renamed. Statues of the late dictator were to be removed from public squares across the land. The delegates also demanded that Stalin's embalmed body be removed from its place beside Lenin in the mausoleum in Red Square and reburied in a simple, unmarked grave at the base of the Kremlin wall.

Khrushchev's hold on power finally seemed secure, but the Soviet Union faced ever more serious problems abroad. Ever since Khrushchev's secret speech, a bitter dispute had been going on between China and the USSR, the world's two largest Communist states. When Khrushchev stepped up his attacks on Stalin and accelerated the pace of reform in Soviet society, the Chinese Communist leadership headed by Mao Zedong could keep silent no longer. The Chinese accused Khrushchev of revisionism—that is, of turning his back on several important doctrines of Marxism-Leninism. Khrushchev reacted angrily and called the Chinese "dogmatists" who cared more about holding onto political power for themselves than they did about truly serving the cause of the working people.

For several years, Soviet and Chinese leaders continued to hurl insults at each other. Communist parties in other countries were forced to choose between the Soviet Union and China. Even though most sided with the Soviets, the division within the world Communist movement was a constant drain on Khrushchev's energy and attention.

Khrushchev also had problems in his relations with the capitalist West. In August 1961 the Communist authorities in East Germany had resorted to building a wall across the center of Berlin to stop their own citizens from fleeing to

Nikita Krushchev greets a crowd during a visit to Armenia in 1960.

the West. The construction of the Berlin Wall was a public relations disaster for Communism.

So too was the Cuban missile crisis. During the summer of 1962, the Soviet Union increased its arms shipments to the government of its ally in Cuba, Fidel Castro. Later, American spy planes discovered that these shipments included sophisticated nuclear missiles. President John F. Kennedy declared that the stationing of Soviet missiles in Cuba, just 90 miles from the United States, was unacceptable. He demanded that the Soviets remove the missiles at once, and he announced a blockade of Cuban waters. The U.S. Navy would stop and search all ships headed toward Cuba, Kennedy said, and if the Soviets attacked any nation in the Western Hemisphere, American retaliation would be massive and swift. The Cuban missile crisis lasted 13 days. Many feared that the world stood at the brink of nuclear war. Finally, on October 28, Khrushchev agreed to dismantle the Soviet missiles in Cuba.

War had been averted, but to many observers, Khrushchev seemed an increasingly weak leader. His unsophisticated, down-to-earth manner, which had once seemed so charming and engaging, now seemed an embarrassment to many Soviet people.

There were problems at home in the USSR as well. The economy was stagnant. Industrial production was in decline. A poor harvest in 1962 had forced the Soviet Union to import wheat for the first time in its history. Conservative Communists believed that Khrushchev's policies undermined the Soviet state, and more radical reformers looked upon Khrushchev's programs as token changes, considering the brutality that still characterized the Soviet system.

In October 1964, Khrushchev's rivals saw another

opportunity to overthrow him. On October 13, while on vacation at his *dacha* on the Black Sea, Khrushchev was summoned to Moscow for a special meeting of the governing presidium. At this special session, Mikhail Suslov, the chief party theoretician, read a long list of charges against Khrushchev. At first, Khrushchev argued with his opponents and defended his record. But as one after another of the members of the presidium rose to agree with Suslov's position, Khrushchev saw that he was completely outnumbered. Reluctantly he agreed to step down, "for reasons of deteriorating health and advanced age."[3]

The next day a meeting of the central committee was called. All members still loyal to Khrushchev were excluded. Those allowed into the meeting unanimously agreed to accept Khrushchev's resignation as party leader and prime minister.

chapter 4

Eras of Stagnation

Following Khrushchev's fall, the central committee declared that one person could no longer hold both the positions of prime minister and party leader. Two men, then, were chosen to succeed the deposed leader. The new prime minister was Aleksei Kosygin, a leader of the Leningrad party, who had first joined the Communist Party in 1927 at the age of 23 in the early years of the Bolshevik regime. The new first secretary of the party was Leonid Brezhnev, who had been born in 1906 into a working-class family in a small city 500 miles south of Moscow. Like Kosygin, Brezhnev had joined the party as a young man and had worked his way up through the ranks. When the members of the presidium looked for someone to replace the outspoken, domineering Khrushchev, the quiet, moderate Brezhnev seemed a good choice. Many believed that Brezhnev was a natural compromiser, a man who would build a genuinely collective leadership rather than concentrating power in his own hands.

For a few years, Brezhnev met these expectations. He labored diligently behind the scenes to eliminate all remaining traces of Khrushchev's reforms. But Brezhnev was also steadily filling all vacancies in the party apparatus with Communists whose primary loyalty was to him. While Kosygin was kept busy overseeing the day-to-day administration of the country, Brezhnev soon came to be acknowledged as the country's real power.

By the time of the Twenty-third Party Congress in 1966, Brezhnev's consolidation of power was nearly complete. At his suggestion the presidium of the party was renamed the Politburo, the same name the group had held in the time of Stalin. Likewise, Brezhnev suggested that his own title be changed from first secretary—the title used by Khrushchev—to the more commanding general secretary— also the title favored by Stalin. The party's high-sounding rhetoric about collective leadership once again gave way to the ambition of a single strong individual.

▼ ▲ ▼

The cornerstones of Brezhnev's rule were stability and control. The Communist Party was again given unrivaled

Leonid Brezhnev and Aleksei Kosygin succeeded deposed leader Nikita Krushchev.

control over every aspect of national life. The *nomenklatura*—the members of the huge central bureaucracy—were assured that the "harebrained schemes" that had characterized Khrushchev's years in office were a thing of the past. If officials did their jobs, met their quotas, and kept their establishments quiet and free of dissent, they would not be bothered by challenging new innovations from Moscow. Indeed, they would be well rewarded for their labors. Party officials were given access to special shops selling all sorts of foreign luxuries unavailable to typical Soviet citizens. Party officials also had access to special health facilities and gymnasiums and their children were admitted to the best schools.

But in spite of stepped-up control under Brezhnev, some people simply refused to conform. Numerous artists and writers who had enjoyed a taste of creative freedom under Khrushchev bristled at Brezhnev's command that the clock be turned back to the years of complete repression. In 1962, Khrushchev had personally approved the publication of Aleksandr Solzhenitsyn's novel *One Day in the Life of Ivan Denisovich* in the official Soviet literary journal *Novy Mir*. Solzhenitsyn's story was a chillingly honest account of life in a labor camp in Siberia. Now, under Brezhnev, Soviet literary authorities balked at publishing any more of Solzhenitsyn's works.

Indeed, repression of "anti-Soviet ideas"—that is, any ideas not in strict conformity with the established party line—was increased. In March 1965 a group of students in the Physics and Mathematics Department at Moscow State University held a conference at which one speaker after another denounced the new repression under Brezhnev. One student even suggested that the official Communist Party newspaper, *Pravda* (which means "truth" in Russian), should be renamed *Lozh* (meaning "lie"). The Soviet government responded to the meeting by tightening controls on students across the USSR.

In September of the same year, two writers—Andrei Sinyavski and Yuli Daniel—were arrested in Moscow and charged with "disseminating slanderous statements against the Soviet state and social system."

At their trial in February 1966, they were, predictably, found guilty. Sinyavski was sentenced to seven years in prison, Daniel to five. To some the trial was a chilling reminder of the show trials of the Stalinist era. But in spite of international protests, repression was stepped up. Restrictions on religious groups were tightened, and church members were harassed and persecuted. Members of ethnic minorities were discriminated against, and the government launched a program to "Russify" life in the 14 non-Russian republics of the USSR. To curb dissent, Soviet medical authorities even declared those who criticized the government mentally incompetent. During Brezhnev's time in power, Soviet mental institutions were filled with thousands of patients whose only illness was daring to speak out against the Communist government.

Brezhnev also dealt ruthlessly with attempts to reform Communism outside of the USSR. In 1968 a group of reformers led by Alexander Dubček gained control of the Communist Party in Czechoslovakia. Press censorship in the country was lifted, and free expression in art and literature was tolerated. The period of openness in Czechoslovakia became known as the Prague Spring.

Brezhnev, however, could not tolerate Dubček's promise of "socialism with a human face." On August 20, 1968, Brezhnev ordered a massive invasion of Czechoslovakia by

Defiant young Czechs carry the nation's flag past a burning Soviet tank shortly after Warsaw Pact troops invaded their country in August 1968.

troops of the Soviet-dominated Warsaw Pact. Dubček and his allies were removed from power, and the new "Brezhnev Doctrine" declared that the Soviet Union would use force if necessary to defend the existence of socialism in Communist states beyond its borders.

▼ ▲ ▼

At home in the Soviet Union Brezhnev also had to deal with economic challenges to Communism. At the beginning of the decade, in 1961, the final communiqué of the Twenty-second Party Congress had described the bright vistas that supposedly lay just over the horizon.

> *In the coming decade [1961–1970] the Soviet Union will create the material and technical basis for communism and will surpass the most powerful and richest capitalist country, the United States. . . . The material well-being of the working people . . . will increase substantially. Everyone will be assured material abundance, while all kolkhozes [collective farms] and sovkhozes [state farms] will become highly productive and highly profitable enterprises. The basic needs of the population for housing will be satisfied; hard physical labor will disappear, and the USSR will become the country with the shortest working day in the world.*[1]

Brezhnev himself later admitted that these predictions had been ridiculously optimistic. Results of the Eighth Five-Year Plan, for 1966 through 1970, lagged far behind projections in almost every field. Nevertheless, Brezhnev continued to insist that the Soviet Union was making great progress along the road to communism. Indeed, Brezhnev declared in 1970 that a new stage in the nation's political journey—a stage he called real socialism—had been achieved.

But beneath the superficial stability of a tightly controlled society, the Soviet Union was approaching a severe crisis. More than 40 years after Stalin had forced collectivization upon the peasants in the name of efficiency and modernization, Soviet agriculture remained strikingly inefficient and old-fashioned. The average American farmer could produce enough food to feed more than 60 people, but the average Soviet farmer produced enough to feed only 8. In spite of official statistics to the contrary, Soviet agricultural production declined steadily throughout the

Brezhnev period. The harvests of 1965, 1967, and 1972 ranked among the worst on record. And the harvest of 1975 was even worse. A nation that had once boasted of being the "breadbasket of Europe" now had to import vast quantities of grain from Canada, the United States, Australia, Argentina, and Brazil.

The situation in industry was not much better. The growth rate of the national economy had slowed noticeably. All of the nation's economic decisions were made in Moscow by officials of *Gosplan*, the large government office of central planning. These officials often had no idea of actual conditions in the enterprises they were charged with overseeing. Soviet consumers continued to face severe shortages of all sorts of goods. The Soviet press ran articles that told of ridiculous bureaucratic errors.

> *In 1969, an article reported how millions of new glasses manufactured by the Ministry of Building Materials cracked when washed in hot water. Just before the start of the 1970 school year, there was a severe shortage of notebooks, drawing pads, rulers, paints, erasers, and plain and colored pencils in schools all across the USSR. School authorities in the Krasnodar region, for example, had ordered 1,860,000 pencils; Gosplan, however, could send them only 285,000. An investigation by* Pravda *discovered the reason for the shortage: every pencil manufactured in the USSR at the time was produced in the same place—an old, dilapidated pencil factory in Siberia.*

In 1971, the national pillow shortage became so severe that sales of the item were limited to newlyweds—who had to show their marriage certificate to prove they were eligible to purchase a pillow![2]

There was also a severe housing shortage. Many Soviet citizens had to wait years just to rent two or three cramped and dreary rooms in a run-down apartment house. Kitchen and bathroom facilities were generally shared with families in other apartments in the building.

And there were many other social problems. Corruption became so widespread that one Soviet lawyer declared that the USSR had become a "kleptocratic state"—that is, a state run by thieves. The health care system was also a mess. Between 1960 and 1975 the average life expectancy of Soviet men and women actually declined. Likewise, between 1970 and 1975, Soviet statistics indicated that the nation's infant mortality rate had increased by one third, to more than three times the rate of the United States or Western Europe. When the rate continued to climb in the late 1970s, the only response of Soviet authorities was to stop publishing the figures.

Alcoholism reached epidemic proportions in the Soviet Union. In Lithuania, for example, consumption of vodka had been estimated at 8 liters per adult in 1963. Ten years later the per capita figure had more than tripled, to 25 liters. The average Lithuanian spent 3 rubles a year on books, and 300 on vodka! These figures were indicative of the situation throughout the country.

▼ ▲ ▼

As more Soviet men and women refused merely to accept the increasingly oppressive nature of their society, the dissident community grew. An extensive network of *samizdat*, or self-published works, circulated throughout the nation. The Brezhnevite authorities responded to this challenge by stepping up surveillance and harassment.

In 1973 a Paris publishing house released the first volume of Aleksandr Solzhenitsyn's monumental work on the Stalinist labor camps, *The Gulag Archipelago*. A few months later, in February 1974, the KGB raided Solzhenitsyn's apartment in Moscow. The author was handcuffed and arrested. Within the next few days, he was charged with treason, tried, convicted, stripped of his citizenship, and expelled from the country. Solzhenitsyn was the first Soviet citizen forcibly deported from the USSR since Trotsky in 1929. He and his family went to live in Switzerland. After a short while there, they moved to Vermont in the United States.

Many other dissidents remained behind. Among their leaders was Andrei Sakharov, a Soviet nuclear scientist whom some called the father of the Soviet Union's hydrogen bomb. Once a highly valued member of Soviet society, Sakharov had been an outspoken critic of the system since the early 1960s. For his outspokenness he was stripped of his high position and placed under constant watch by the KGB. But Sakharov refused to remain silent, and in 1975 he was awarded the Nobel Peace Prize for his work in defense of human rights. In January 1980, however, the Soviet government forced Sakharov to move from Moscow to Gorki, a city nearly 300 miles from the capital. In spite of his isolation in Gorki, Sakharov worked hard to keep the Soviet human rights movement alive.

As the Brezhnev years dragged on, the entire Soviet nation seemed mired in stagnation. A deep mood of cynicism and despair seemed to pervade all aspects of national life.

As Brezhnev grew older and his health began to fail, rumors circulated that the general secretary (who after 1977 also held the largely ceremonial post of president of the USSR) was becoming senile. A popular joke compared the leadership styles of Stalin, Khrushchev, and Brezhnev:

> *A train carrying the three Soviet leaders stalls somewhere on the vast Soviet frontier. People turn to Stalin, the senior leader, and ask how to get the train going again. Without hesitation, the Soviet dictator replies: "Shoot the engineers. Exile the crew. Get someone new." A short while later, however, the train stalls again. Now, the people turn to Khrushchev, who pardons the people exiled by Stalin and gets the train moving again. But then, it stalls a third time. The people turn to Brezhnev, and ask him what to do. Brezhnev thinks for a moment, and then issues his orders: "Just pull down the shades, and pretend that we're moving."*[3]

▼ ▲ ▼

On November 10, 1982, Leonid Brezhnev died of a heart attack at his home in Moscow. Again, after 17 years, there would be a power struggle within the Soviet hierarchy.

There were two chief contenders: Konstantin Chernenko, Brezhnev's closest friend and advisor, and Yuri Andropov, former chief of the KGB. In spite of his closeness to Brezhnev, Chernenko seemed to have little to recommend him. He was already 71 years old in 1982 but

Konstantin Chernenko (*right*) receiving the Order of Lenin from Leonid Brezhnev in 1981

had been a full member of the ruling Politburo for only four years. His long career in the party was particularly undistinguished, and he seemed a man of little charm, no special skill, and a most limited imagination.

Andropov, on the other hand, had been part of the Communist hierarchy for almost 30 years. Following his posting as Soviet ambassador to Hungary from 1953 to 1957, he had been named to the central committee. In 1967, twelve years before Chernenko, he became a member of the Politburo. Andropov quickly emerged as the obviously superior candidate and, on November 12, 1982, was named the new Communist general secretary.

Andropov had been waiting years for his chance to lead. He wasted no time in launching extensive, well-publicized national campaigns—against corruption, drunkenness, and the abuse of power. Thousands of Brezhnev loyalists were removed from office. Brezhnev's own daughter, Galina, was implicated in a diamond-smuggling ring, and her husband was sentenced to a long prison term for taking bribes.

But in spite of his talk of reform, Andropov was no friend of democracy or human rights. On the contrary, the former KGB chief stepped up persecution of the dissident community. Even tighter restrictions were placed on Sakharov and other human-rights activists. The number of Soviet Jews allowed to emigrate to Israel was sharply cut back. In his speeches to the Soviet people, Andropov consistently stressed discipline, rather than reform, as the chief means of revitalizing Soviet society.

Meanwhile, relations with the West steadily worsened. The Soviet invasion of Afghanistan under Brezhnev in December 1979 had brought the era of détente, or more relaxed relations, between East and West to a screeching halt. Rather than withdrawing from Afghanistan, however, Andropov beefed up Soviet involvement. Then on the night of August 31, 1983, the Soviet air force shot down a South Korean passenger jet that had strayed into Soviet airspace. Nearly 300 civilians were killed, many of them Americans. Relations between the two superpowers descended to the lowest point since the Cuban missile crisis. The huge stockpiles of nuclear weapons on both sides increased fears of a nuclear holocaust.

For all the high goals he had established for himself, Andropov accomplished very little. Even at the time of his election as general secretary, he was in poor health. In August 1983, Andropov disappeared from public view. Official Soviet reports said he had a cold. In reality he was suffering from acute kidney failure. In spite of medical treatment, Andropov's condition worsened, and on February 9, 1984, the Soviet press announced his death, after only 15 months in office.

Now at last it was Chernenko's turn to lead the country. True to expectations, Brezhnev's close protégé proved an utterly uninspired national leader. Although Chernenko paid lip service to Andropov's campaigns for discipline and against corruption, the campaigns were, in reality, quietly allowed to die out.

But Chernenko had grandiose plans of his own. In November 1984, the central committee adopted a "Program for Land Improvement," which promised a solution to the country's nagging agricultural problems. Among the program's more ambitious ideas was a plan to reverse the flow of the Irtysh, Lena, and Ob rivers in Siberia from north to south so that they might be used to irrigate farmlands beyond the Urals and in western Siberia.

Many international scientists expressed grave concern about the plan. There was no way of gauging with any certainty the effects of such a large-scale tampering with nature. Many believed that the severe reduction of water flowing into the northern Arctic Ocean that would result might significantly lower the ocean's temperature. The effects would be devastating and would be felt all over the world.

But, like Andropov before him, Chernenko would not live to see his grand plans implemented. From the very start of his term as general secretary, it was clear that his health too was in decline. Increasingly, Chernenko relied upon the younger men in the Politburo, especially Mikhail Gorbachev, to carry out his official functions. Although many even began to call Gorbachev the party's second secretary, others doubted whether Gorbachev, who had been a strong supporter of Yuri Andropov, would succeed Chernenko as general secretary.

Gorbachev's main rival was Viktor Grishin, who had headed the Moscow party organization since 1967. He was of the same generation as Chernenko and had proven himself a dedicated Brezhnev protégé. In October 1984, Chernenko had marked Grishin's seventieth birthday by awarding him the Order of Lenin, the Soviet Union's highest decoration. He had also hinted at the time that Grishin was the kind of man he would like to see as his successor.

As Chernenko's health continued to decline, this preference became clearer. In February 1985, Chernenko was too ill to read his own election speech. Grishin read it for him. A few days later, viewers of Soviet television watched as Chernenko, extremely ill, cast his ballot. The room in which Chernenko voted was obviously not a regular polling station. Most people assumed that it was a hastily converted hospital room. As Chernenko struggled to place his ballot in the collection box, his loyal assistant Grishin stood at his side to help. A few days later the two were seen together on the evening news again. This time Grishin was said to be congratulating Chernenko on his unanimous victory in the just-concluded elections.

On March 10, 1985, after only 13 months in office Konstantin Chernenko died in Moscow at the age of 74. He had served as Soviet leader for an even shorter time than Andropov. The Politburo met immediately to choose Chernenko's successor. A decision was made quickly, and as representatives of the Communist Party stood before reporters the next day, no one could have imagined that they were announcing, in effect, the name of the man who would be the last leader of the Soviet state.

chapter 5

Gorbachev: Like a Breath Of Fresh Air

At first, Grishin seemed to have an advantage over Gorbachev in the struggle to succeed Chernenko. Former Brezhnev protégés seemed to hold a clear majority in the Politburo. Four of the ten members, including Gorbachev himself, had been closely identified with Andropov. But when the eldest member of the Politburo, Foreign Minister Andrei Gromyko, who had been appointed to his position by Khrushchev in 1957, nominated Gorbachev to be the party's new leader, it was obvious that the fight would be a very close one.

In nominating Gorbachev for the top post, Gromyko reminded the other Politburo members that Gorbachev had been, in effect, the second in command throughout much of Chernenko's time in office. Indeed, during the last months of Chernenko's illness, Gorbachev had chaired the meetings of the secretariat and the Politburo. "He demonstrated that he is brilliant, without any exaggeration . . ." Gromyko continued. "This is a man of principles, a man of strong convictions. . . . He has a great skill for organizing people, and for finding a common language with them." Then, as though both to emphasize Gorbachev's strength and to disarm critics who claimed that Gorbachev was too soft, the old-school Communist is said to have concluded, "Comrades, this man has a nice smile, but he's got iron teeth."[1]

Gromyko's message was clear. It was time for the old guard to pass the leadership of the party to the next generation. His words in favor of Gorbachev seemed to carry the day, and when a vote was taken, Mikhail Sergeyevich Gorbachev was elected as the Soviet general secretary.

▼ ▲ ▼

On assuming the top position, Gorbachev learned for the first time just how severe the problems in the USSR were. There could be no continuation of business as usual, he told his fellow Communists. There was a need for everyone, especially those in leadership positions, to work harder. There was a need to modernize Soviet industry. If the country was to keep its position in the world economy, a scientific and technological revolution must be launched as well. Only then could a higher standard of living be guaranteed for all the Soviet people.

General Secretary Gorbachev wasted no time in bringing his ideas to the public. Just a few days before the April meeting, Gorbachev had stunned the citizens of Moscow by arriving unannounced for a visit to the Proletarskii section of the city. The visit was the first of many walkabouts among common Soviet citizens that Gorbachev would make. He visited several factories and discussed conditions with the workers. He visited a supermarket, joked with schoolchildren, and dropped by to visit the apartment of a young family. Soviet citizens viewing scenes of the walkabout on the evening news could hardly believe their eyes.

Gorbachev meets with workers in the Proletarskii section of Moscow.

In May, Gorbachev traveled to Leningrad, the second largest city in the Soviet Union. His visit marked the first time in more than two years that a Soviet leader had been well enough to travel beyond Moscow. Gorbachev soon made it clear that this visit would not be like those that had taken place in the past. He told the Leningrad party chief, Lev Zaikov, that he was not interested in visiting a few carefully chosen factories. Rather, he wanted to visit places where the "real" people of Leningrad worked and shopped and lived, just as he had in Moscow. The people of Leningrad greeted Gorbachev warmly. They were excited about his plans for change and felt gratified that one of their leaders actually cared enough to ask their views on matters of importance.

On his first night in Leningrad, Gorbachev spoke before a gathering of members of the city's Communist Party. The Soviet Union required nothing less than complete *perestroika*—"restructuring"—Gorbachev declared. This restructuring would require an "immense mobilization" of the whole society, he continued. It would be a task as demanding as the war against Hitler's Germany had been.

Gorbachev obviously meant business, and wherever he went the Soviet people responded with a great outpouring of support. In June he visited the large Ukrainian cities of Kiev and Dnepropetrovsk. The next month he traveled to the Byelorussian Republic and spoke before several large gatherings. Trips were also planned to Siberia and Kazakhstan in central Asia.

All along the way the Soviet press gave extensive coverage to the energetic general secretary. When Gorbachev was in Leningrad, the nightly news program *Vremya* dedicated most of its broadcast to his visit. One hundred million Soviet citizens watched as a woman shouted to Gorbachev, "You should be closer to the people!" "How can I be any closer?" the general secretary responded, barely visible amid the throng of Leningraders.[2] The crowd on screen roared its approval, and across the USSR, people shook their heads in amazement at the humor and zest of their new leader and his polished, intelligent wife, Raisa, who accompanied him on all his journeys.

Gorbachev's growing popular support gave him confidence to make further changes. In July, Andrei Gromyko stepped down from his post as foreign minister and was given the largely ceremonial position of chairman of the Supreme Soviet. He was replaced as foreign minister by

Eduard Shevardnadze, the head of the Communist Party in the Soviet republic of Georgia. Over the years, Shevardnadze's efforts to root out corruption and incompetence within the Georgian party had attracted much attention. Shevardnadze was also named to the ruling Politburo, and two other supporters of reform, Lev Zaikov and Boris Yeltsin, were given seats on the party's secretariat.

In August, Aleksandr Yakovlev, a close personal friend of Gorbachev who had served as the Soviet ambassador to Canada, was named head of the central committee's propaganda department. Yakovlev's task would be to form Soviet public opinion in favor of the new party line of the Gorbachev era. In late September another reformer, Nikolai Ryzhkov, was named prime minister.

▼ ▲ ▼

Gorbachev moved quickly to reinstitute several of Andropov's programs that Chernenko had let lapse during his time in power. With great fanfare he also announced an extensive new program to fight alcohol abuse. One Soviet official estimated that alcohol abuse was a factor in more than two thirds of the crimes committed in the USSR as well as in 98 percent of all murders, 40 percent of all divorces, 50 percent of all accidents, and 63 percent of all drownings. Approximately 90 percent of the inmates of juvenile correction colonies had been sentenced for crimes committed while intoxicated. Between 1964 and 1985, the Soviet Union's death rate had risen from 6.9 per thousand to 10.8. Authorities believed that the chief factor in this huge jump was the increased consumption of alcohol during the same period.

While previous Soviet leaders had chosen to ignore the problem, Gorbachev decided to attack it head-on. On May 16, 1985, the legal drinking age in the USSR was raised from 18 to 21. Two thirds of all state liquor stores were closed, and many state-owned distilleries were converted to plants for manufacturing soft drinks. Alcoholic beverages were removed from the shelves of ordinary food stores. Liquor stores and restaurants were banned from selling alcohol before two o'clock in the afternoon, and bartenders and waiters were ordered not to serve more than two drinks per customer. The fine for public drunkenness was increased by 1,000 percent.

At first Gorbachev's antialcohol campaign was greeted with great enthusiasm. People across the country vowed to keep their communities alcohol-free. Farmers in the wine-producing regions in the south of the country ripped out their vineyards and planted other crops to replace them. Many Soviet citizens were especially impressed when Gorbachev banned the serving of alcohol at all official banquets and receptions. Because of his personal preference for mineral water rather than vodka, General Secretary Gorbachev became known as Mineral Water Secretary Gorbachev.

But it was not long before the title "Mineral Water Secretary"—originally intended as a sign of affection—became a nickname of disdain. As the availability of vodka was restricted, long lines, known as Gorbachev's nooses, soon formed outside of the few state liquor stores that remained open.

People searched out other means of satisfying their need for alcohol. Many bought huge quantities of sugar in order to make their own homemade vodka. When the supply of sugar in state-owned grocery stores was almost depleted, the government had to impose strict rationing. Desperate alcoholics unable to buy legal vodka or make their own soon began drinking cologne, paint thinner, industrial solvent, even brake fluid—anything that contained alcohol.

▼ ▲ ▼

But in spite of the setbacks suffered in the campaign against alcohol, Gorbachev made significant progress in other areas during his first year in office. At the time that Gorbachev came to power in March 1985, the Soviet Union was spending approximately one quarter of its national income on the production of weapons and the maintenance of its armed forces. Gorbachev realized that these huge expenditures might eventually bankrupt the Soviet economy if they were not reduced drastically. But in order to cut back on the military budget, Gorbachev had to find a way to reduce tensions between the world's two superpowers.

Relations between the USSR and the United States were at a low point. Because of the Soviet invasion of Afghanistan, the U.S. Congress had refused to ratify the second Strategic Arms Limitation Treaty (SALT II). In March 1983 the president of the United States, Ronald Reagan, had denounced the Soviet Union as an "evil empire" intent upon world domination. Later that same year, the Soviet representatives walked out of the arms limitations talks in Geneva, Switzerland, to protest deployment of American nuclear missiles in West Germany.

The Geneva talks had finally been revived in February 1985, only a month before the death of Chernenko. After taking office, Gorbachev moved quickly to exploit the opportunity at hand. Through his representatives at

Gorbachev: Like a Breath of Fresh Air 65

Geneva, he signaled that he was willing to enter into direct negotiations with President Reagan.

Reagan accepted Gorbachev's offer. In July 1985 the foreign ministry of the USSR and the U.S. State Department announced that their nation's leaders would meet for a summit conference in Geneva that coming November. In Geneva, both Reagan and Gorbachev proposed cutting their nations' nuclear stockpiles by one half.

Even more important than the particular agreements reached at Geneva was the atmosphere of hope that the summit created. As they were preparing to conclude their meetings, the American president remarked to the Soviet general secretary, "I bet the hard-liners in both our

President Ronald Reagan and Soviet leader Mikhail Gorbachev shake hands at the start of summit talks in Geneva.

countries are bleeding when we shake hands."[3] Indeed, the willingness of these two very different world leaders to negotiate with each other in an honest and straightforward manner represented a refreshing change from the distrust that had come to characterize United States-Soviet relations over the past decades.

▼ ▲ ▼

The main business facing Gorbachev when he returned from Geneva included preparations for the Twenty-seventh Congress of the Communist Party of the Soviet Union, which opened in Moscow on February 25, 1986. In his five-hour speech convening the Congress, Gorbachev presented a more detailed vision for restructuring Soviet society.

Not only did the Soviet economy have to change, Gorbachev stressed, but there was also a need to encourage integrity and honesty at all levels of society. Only through *glasnost*—"openness"—could the Soviet people face the mistakes of the past honestly and meet the challenges of the future confidently.

Gorbachev's promises of *glasnost* were soon to be put to a severe test. Just after one o'clock in the morning on April 26, 1986, there was an explosion in one of the reactors at the Chernobyl nuclear power plant, 50 miles north of the Ukrainian capital Kiev. Huge amounts of nuclear radiation were released into the atmosphere. Farmland and drinking water in vast areas of the Ukrainian, Byelorussian, Lithuanian, and Latvian Soviet republics were contaminated. Thousands of people would eventually die from the effects of the accident.

Workers monitor radiation after the Chernobyl nuclear accident.

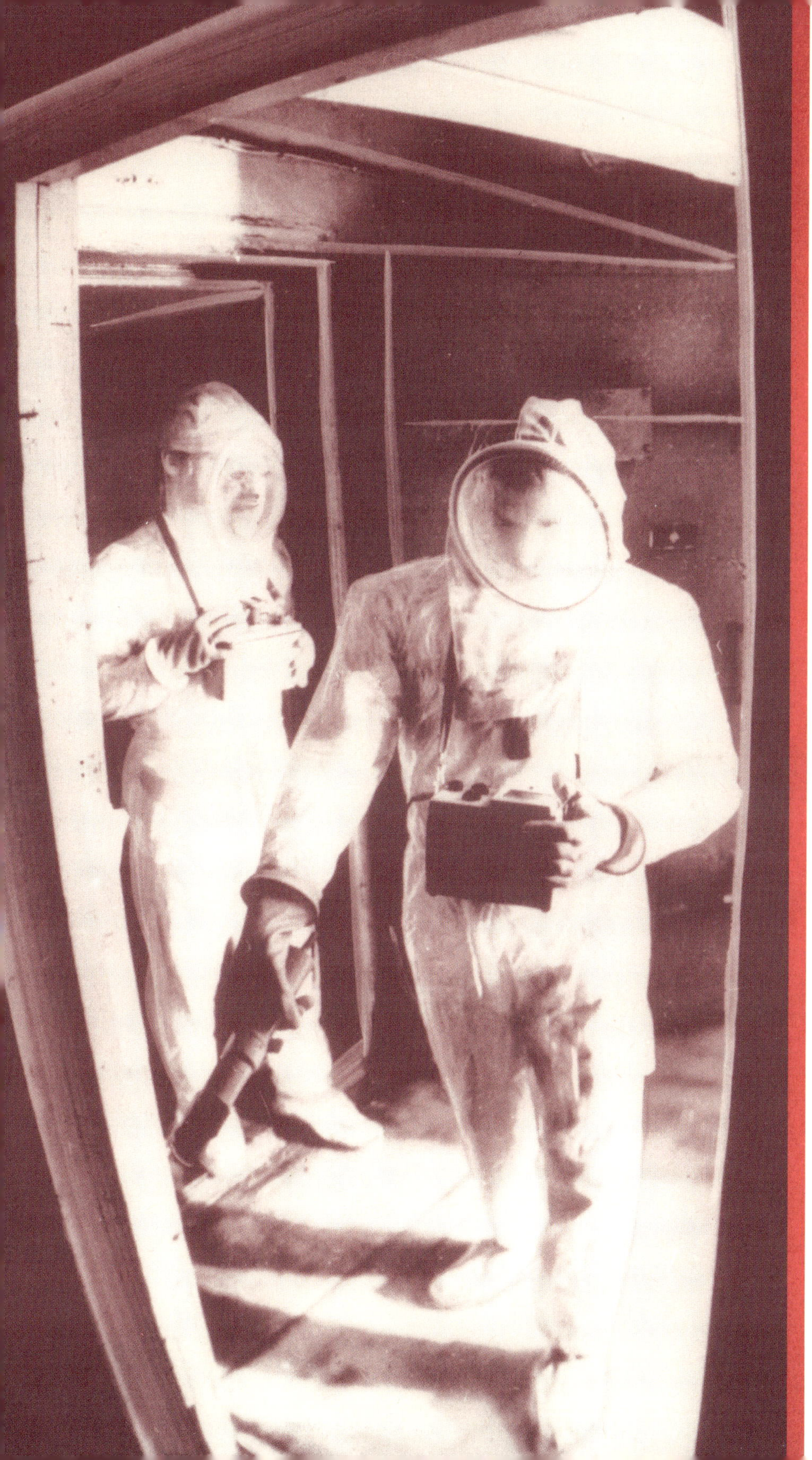

Gorbachev's first response to Chernobyl was to do nothing. The Soviet government waited three days before admitting that an accident had even occurred, and it did so only when monitors in Finland and Sweden reported abnormally high levels of radiation in the atmosphere. Authorities also waited three days before evacuating the towns in the immediate vicinity of the power plant. Ten days passed before the government offered any detailed explanation of what had happened, and even then many questions were left unanswered. Finally, on May 14—nearly three weeks after the catastrophe—Mikhail Gorbachev addressed the nation about the disaster.

But instead of taking the opportunity to speak honestly about the situation at Chernobyl, Gorbachev attacked those who had dared to criticize his government's response. "Political figures and the mass media of certain countries, especially the United States . . . used the Chernobyl accident as a jumping-off point for an unrestrained anti-Soviet campaign," Gorbachev seethed. Many of the reports coming from the West about the extent of the Chernobyl disaster—about the hundreds of thousands of casualties and the large-scale ecological devastation—were, Gorbachev said, "a mountain of lies."[4]

As one foreign observer lamented, Gorbachev's address on Chernobyl "could have come from the mouth of any one of [his] predecessors from Stalin to Chernenko. . . . It was one of Gorbachev's worst moments."[5] Many observers—both inside and outside the Soviet Union—now realized that there was still a very long way to go on the road toward glasnost and perestroika.

chapter 6

Hard-Liners vs. Reformers

In the wake of the criticism that followed Chernobyl, the pace of *glasnost* accelerated. Numerous articles critical of the government response to Chernobyl appeared in the Soviet press. Many of these articles openly took issue with government attempts to downplay the effects of the meltdown. By the summer of 1986, several of the country's leading magazines and newspapers were under the management of editors sympathetic to *glasnost*.

A new spirit of openness characterized the Soviet film industry as well. Films made years before but repressed by government censors were finally released. Perhaps the most important of the new films was *Repentance*, a drama by the Georgian filmmaker Tengiz Abuladze about the Stalinist terror. Abuladze had made the film in the early 1980s with the support of Georgian Communist Party leader Eduard Shevardnadze. When Shevardnadze became foreign minister in 1986, he urged Gorbachev to allow the film's release.

Gorbachev agreed to view *Repentance* privately and was deeply moved. Abuladze's story of persecution and terror struck deeply in Gorbachev's own memory. He remembered how his own grandfather had been arrested by Stalin's agents and sent to the labor camps. As the film ended and Gorbachev rose to leave, he told one of his aides, "Make sure that enough copies are made so that everyone in the country can see it."[1]

▼ ▲ ▼

In October 1986, Reagan and Gorbachev met in Reykjavík, Iceland, for their second summit conference. Hopes for the Reykjavík meetings ran very high. On the first day of the summit, Gorbachev announced his acceptance of Reagan's proposal to cut the nuclear arsenals of both superpowers by one half and then proposed even more extensive cutbacks. The next day the American side agreed to extend for ten years the treaty limiting the development of antiballistic missiles (ABMs). In private meetings, Reagan then raised the stakes even higher. He proposed that both sides dismantle *all* of their nuclear weapons over a ten-year period. Gorbachev quickly agreed to the American proposal.

But then the Reykjavík agreement collapsed. Gorbachev insisted that the United States halt its development of the Strategic Defense Initiative (SDI, or Star Wars, as it was commonly called). Reagan adamantly refused to even consider Gorbachev's proposal. Deployment of SDI was the cornerstone of his administration's defense policy; it was the one thing on which he would not compromise. "I made a promise to the American people that I would not trade away Star Wars," the American president told the Soviet leader.[2] Then there would be no Reykjavík agreement, Gorbachev bluntly replied, and he stormed out of the room.

The Reykjavík summit adjourned in a mood of deep

Hard-liners vs. Reformers 71

disappointment. Many feared that Soviet-American relations would deteriorate once again. Future events, however, would demonstrate that Reykjavík represented merely a temporary setback along the road to full-scale disarmament.

▼ ▲ ▼

On his return from the summit, Gorbachev decided to send a clear signal of his willingness to make real changes in Soviet society. Late one night in December 1986, KGB agents arrived at Andrei Sakharov's apartment in Gorki. They were there, they told Sakharov, to install a telephone —something that the Soviet dissident had been denied for the seven years that he had lived in internal exile. The next

President Reagan and Soviet leader Gorbachev have a few final words after the collapse of their summit meeting in Reykjavík.

Andrei Sakharov speaks to reporters on his return to Moscow.

afternoon the telephone rang; Gorbachev was on the line. A decision had been made to allow Sakharov to return to Moscow, the general secretary said. "Go back to your patriotic work," Gorbachev told the exiled scientist.[3] By the end of the month, Sakharov was back in Moscow.

The pace of *glasnost* continued to pick up. Works by long-banned authors began to appear in Soviet bookstores. A new Russian translation of the anti-Soviet satire *1984* by George Orwell was an immediate best-seller. A government commission was established to oversee publication of *Doctor Zhivago* by the Soviet Nobel prize winner Boris Pasternak. The literary journal *Oktyabr* published the anti-Stalinist poem "Requiem" by Anna Akmatova. "Requiem" was a work well known abroad, but it had never been published in the USSR. Similarly the historical novel *Children of the Arbat* by Anatoli Rybakov, a frank description of life during Stalinist times, was published in 1987—21 years after it had first been banned by government censors.

▼ ▲ ▼

Gorbachev's position seemed strong and secure. In early August 1987, he left Moscow for a vacation at his country house in the Crimea. He would not return to the capital for seven weeks. During that time, rumors as to his whereabouts spread. He was gravely ill, some said. According to others, he had had a nervous breakdown. Some believed Gorbachev was plotting a dictatorial takeover. Still others claimed that he had been forced from power by Stalinist hard-liners.

In reality, Gorbachev was writing a book, *Perestroika: New Thinking for Our Country and the World*. In *Perestroika*, Gorbachev presented his vision of a peaceful world: "This world is . . . one whole," Gorbachev wrote. "We are all passengers aboard one ship, the Earth, and we must not allow it to be wrecked. There will be no second Noah's Ark."[4] Of the restructuring under way in his own land, Gorbachev remarked, "*Perestroika* is no whim on the part of some ambitious individuals or a group of leaders. . . . *Perestroika* is an urgent necessity. . . . This society is ripe for change. It has long been yearning for it."[5]

Indeed, change was sweeping the Soviet land. A wide array of new organizations had sprung up, advocating everything from new religions to the brewing of homemade beer. Some groups had explicitly political aims. The Memorial Society supported construction of a monument to the victims of Stalin. Another group, Pamyat, originally formed to further appreciation of Russian culture and literature, soon took extremely nationalistic, anti-Semitic stands. Yet, though many Russians found Pamyat's views objectionable, its membership continued to grow. In May 1987 the group was able to organize a large march through the streets of downtown Moscow.

▼ ▲ ▼

Throughout 1987, there were also signs of widening division within the Communist Party. Within the ruling Politburo two distinct factions had formed. One group, the reformers, favored increased political freedom, while the other faction, the hard-liners, wanted a return to the discipline and order of traditional Communism. Soon two individuals in the Politburo—Boris Yeltsin and Yegor Ligachev—came to be viewed as the chief representatives of these different positions.

Soon after returning from vacation, in October 1987, Gorbachev called a meeting of the central committee to review the progress of perestroika. Following Gorbachev's report, Yeltsin, head of the Moscow party, delivered a scathing attack on the hard-liners in general and on Ligachev in particular. Even though perestroika was supposedly well under way, Yeltsin said, Ligachev and the hard-liners were dragging their feet. "Nothing has changed in the style of work of either the Secretariat of the Central

Committee or of Comrade Ligachev," Yeltsin declared. As a result, people were growing impatient, and their faith in perestroika had begun to ebb.

Then Yeltsin turned his attack on Gorbachev himself.

> *Recently there has been a noticeable increase in what I can only call adulation of the General Secretary by certain full members of the Politburo. I consider this to be impermissible, particularly now that we are introducing properly democratic forms of relations among one another, truly comradely relationships. The tendency to adulation is absolutely unacceptable. To criticize to people's faces—yes, that is necessary—but not to develop a taste for adulation, which can become the norm again, can become a "cult of personality." We cannot permit this . . .*[6]

Gorbachev immediately accused Yeltsin of trying "to fight the central committee." Then Ligachev defended himself and denied both that there was a problem in his relations with Yeltsin and that Gorbachev was receiving inordinate praise. By the end of the meeting, two dozen central committee members, including many leading reformers, rose to denounce Yeltsin's remarks. His speech had been "politically wrong and morally wrong," Aleksandr Yakovlev said. Foreign Minister Eduard Shevardnadze called Yeltsin's speech "a betrayal of the party."[7] Finally, at Gorbachev's urging, a decision on Yeltsin's fate was postponed until after the ceremonies on November 2 commemorating the seventieth anniversary of the Bolshevik revolution.

Two weeks later, with the anniversary commemoration out of the way, Gorbachev dealt firmly with Yeltsin. In spite of the fact that Yeltsin was in the hospital suffering from exhaustion, Gorbachev demanded an emergency meeting of the Moscow party committee. On the morning of November 11, 1987, he telephoned the hospital. "You must come and see me for a short while, Boris Nikolayevich," Gorbachev said calmly. "After that, perhaps we will go and attend the plenum of the Moscow city committee together." Yeltsin protested that he was hospitalized on doctors' orders. But Gorbachev pressed on. "Don't worry," he told Yeltsin. "The doctors will help you get up."[8]

Heavily sedated and barely able to walk, Yeltsin was helped from his bed, led to a waiting car, and driven to the party headquarters in downtown Moscow. There, Gorbachev and the rest of the Politburo, as well as the members of the Moscow party committee, were waiting for him. Gorbachev spoke first. Yeltsin's conduct at the October 21 meeting had been "politically immature and extremely confused and contradictory,"[9] Gorbachev said. His speech had done a disservice to the cause of *perestroika*. Then he opened the meeting to general discussion.

For several hours, Yeltsin was the object of a torrent of hostility. One committee member after another rose to denounce Yeltsin's "incompetence" and "immaturity" and to condemn the way he had "stabbed the party in the back." Only one speaker, A. S. Yeliseyev, a former cosmonaut who was head of a large technical college in the capital, dared to speak in defense of Yeltsin.

Utterly exhausted by the ordeal, Yeltsin could utter but a few words in response. He apologized that his own ambitions had gotten in the way of his doing his job in Moscow. He apologized to the party—and to Gorbachev—for the trouble he had caused. The city committee then voted unanimously to remove Boris Yeltsin from his position as head of the

Moscow Communist Party. A short while later Yeltsin was removed from the Politburo as well.

▼ ▲ ▼

The sacking of Yeltsin gave Ligachev and the hard-liners confidence to mount a direct challenge to *glasnost* and *perestroika*. In March 1988, Gorbachev left Moscow on a visit to Yugoslavia. In his absence, control of the party passed to Ligachev, the deputy party leader, who quickly moved to consolidate his position. He used his temporary position at the top of the party to have a long article by Nina Andreyava, an obscure chemistry instructor at Leningrad Technical Institute, placed prominently in newspapers throughout the country.

In her article, "I Cannot Forsake Principles," Andreyava sternly criticized the direction the country was taking. She lashed out at "modernistic tendencies" like rock-and-roll music, anti-Soviet books and plays, and religious publications from the West. All these things, Andreyava said, created an atmosphere of "confusion" among her students. The country should not turn its back on the "glorious example" of Soviet history, the teacher from Leningrad declared. She defended Brezhnev and even lauded Stalin as a great "trailblazer" of socialism.

Some later claimed that Ligachev himself—or perhaps one of his assistants—had actually written the piece credited to Andreyava. Certainly the deputy leader had used his position to give the article the widest possible circulation. Publication of "I Cannot Forsake Principles" alarmed Soviet reformers. Many feared that Gorbachev's position was in danger and that a new conservative government would soon reverse the changes that had already been made.

After his return from Yugoslavia, Gorbachev chose not to move against Ligachev at once. But at a meeting of the Politburo in early April, Gorbachev condemned the Andreyava article and criticized Ligachev for the part he had played in having it published. The general secretary demanded that the Politburo authorize Aleksandr Yakovlev, the Soviet propaganda chief, to publish a stern rebuttal. If the Politburo refused to answer Andreyava, Gorbachev concluded, he would immediately resign. The general secretary then rose from his seat, announced that he would await their decision at his home outside of Moscow, and left the room.

While many of the Politburo members present had serious concerns about where Gorbachev's reforms were headed, none wanted the responsibility for charting a different course. They realized that the country had changed too much to return to the old ways and that there now seemed no alternative to *perestroika*. Should Gorbachev simply step down, there would be widespread confusion throughout the land, perhaps even open revolts in the streets. The Politburo authorized Yakovlev to respond to Andreyava.

In his article Yakovlev condemned "blind, die-hard dogmatist[s]" who wished to return to the "nostalgia" of the Stalinist past. *Glasnost* was not an easy process, Yakovlev wrote, but the modernization of socialism required genuine democracy. To return to the ways of the past would be to allow socialism to stagnate and eventually wither. The Soviet people were confused, Yakovlev concluded, because in the past their leaders had talked about the great victories of socialism while doing little to improve the day-to-day lives of the working people.

On December 1, 1988, the Soviet legislature approved Gorbachev's plan for "democratization"—the third facet of his program for change. "There can be no socialism without elections," Gorbachev had said.[10] Under his new plan, more than half of the seats in a newly created national legislature, the Congress of People's Deputies, were to be chosen in free and open elections. For the first time in Soviet history, voters would be able to choose from more than one candidate. However, there would not be contested elections for every seat in the new Congress. Under Gorbachev's plan, 750 of the 2,250 delegates to the Congress would be appointed directly by the Communist Party and its affiliated organizations.

For almost three months an unprecedented electoral campaign riveted the attention of people all across the Soviet Union. While most of the candidates running for election were Communist Party members, there were also a large number of independent candidates. Chief among these was Andrei Sakharov. Sakharov remained as uncompromising and outspoken as ever. He complained that the pace of Gorbachev's reforms was too slow and must be speeded up. As election day approached, Sakharov was given an excellent chance of gaining a seat in the new legislature.

Boris Yeltsin's prospects of winning elections were good as well. Since his removal from the party leadership, Yeltsin's popularity had skyrocketed. People in nearly 200 different districts across Russia had nominated him to run for election to the new Congress. Finally Yeltsin had chosen to run for a seat representing the city of Moscow. Yeltsin's opponent was Yevgeny Brakov, the director of the Moscow factory that produced elite Zil automobiles for

People show support for Yeltsin.

members of the party hierarchy. While Brakov campaigned as a loyal supporter of Gorbachev and *perestroika*, voters continued to identify him with the unpopular policies and privileges of the past.

When Soviet voters went to the polls on March 26, they made their discontent very clear. All across the Soviet Union, radical reformers gained seats in the new Congress. Members of the Academy of Sciences elected the dissident Sakharov as one of their representatives. Boris Yeltsin gained 89 percent of the vote in his race against Brakov. Historian Roy Medvedev, who had been among the first to denounce the crimes of Stalin, was also elected to the new Congress, as was the famous Russian poet Yevgeny Yevtushenko.

Nationalist candidates also made a strong showing. In the Ukraine, candidates loyal to the national Communist Party were defeated by staunch Ukrainian nationalists. Huge victories were also enjoyed by pro-independence movements in the Baltic states of Estonia, Latvia, and Lithuania and in the small western republic of Moldavia.

All across the country, in the three largest cities of Moscow, Leningrad, and Kiev; in Asian cities like Alma-Ata, Yarolslavl, and Kuibyshev; even in the remote Siberian city of Tomsk, local party leaders were defeated in stunning upsets. Of 399 party officials who had run unopposed, nearly half were denied seats in the Congress when voters in their districts took the time to cross out their names on the paper ballots.

All together, radical reformers had been victorious in about 400 individual contests. Even before the Congress officially convened, these non-Communist deputies started meeting together to forge a common strategy. At first they called themselves the March Coalition, in honor of the March elections in which they had been elected. Later they would officially name themselves the Inter-Regional Group. The Inter-Regional Group would still be a definite minority in the 2,250-seat Congress, in control of fewer than one fifth of all of the seats. But now, when this bloc of independent-minded, popularly chosen delegates chose to speak as one, their voice would certainly be heard. For the first time since the Leninist takeover in 1917, the Communist Party faced an organized opposition.

chapter 7

Winters of Discontent

In May 1989, Mikhail Gorbachev returned to Moscow from an official visit to China. Everywhere he turned, there seemed to be severe problems that demanded attention. It was clear that the USSR was entering a difficult period in its history. Protests were still being heard over events in the Georgian capital, Tbilisi, where a month earlier security forces had killed 20 people while suppressing a peaceful demonstration. Nationalist demonstrations were now taking place in cities all across the USSR, from the Baltic capitals in the north to the steppes of central Asia in the south. Armenian and Azerbaijani nationalists were battling each other over control of the disputed region of Nagorno-Karabakh. Nationalist clashes racked the Moldavian republic as well.

The 1988 grain harvest had been the worst in three years. Other sectors of the national economy were not doing very well either. The centralized economic system was being dismantled, and local managers were being given increased control. But these officials, who had risen to their positions under the old Soviet system, had never received training to prepare them for work under the new one. In some places, production had simply come to a halt as confused managers awaited further instructions from Moscow. Increasingly, dissatisfied workers were striking to protest the deteriorating economic situation. In the summer of 1989, half a million coal miners in Siberia and the Ukraine were threatening to walk off their jobs unless their demands for higher wages and better working conditions were met. Without a steady supply of coal, many of the largest plants in the country would be forced to shut down.

While many rank-and-file Soviet citizens had greeted Gorbachev's early proposals for reform with enthusiasm, many now felt that they had very little to show for four years of *perestroika*. Indeed, the lines in state-owned stores were longer, and the shelves emptier, than they had been even during the Brezhnev "era of stagnation." Popular sentiment was summed up in a little poem that was making its way around Moscow.

> *Sausage prices twice as high,*
> *Where's the vodka for us to buy?*
> *All we do is sit at home,*
> *Watching Gorby drone and drone.*[1]

In the midst of these severe problems, the Congress of People's Deputies convened in Moscow on May 25. Gorbachev attempted to dominate the proceedings, but the newly elected reformers were also intent upon using the Congress to press their demands. The debates of the Congress were broadcast live on Soviet television. Day after day, 200 million people across the Soviet Union watched as opposition deputies criticized one thing after another: the slow pace of *perestroika*, mismanagement of the economy, the continued power of high party officials, the use of deadly force to disperse peaceful demonstrators, the

1979 invasion of Afghanistan, continued Soviet domination of the Baltic states. One deputy even rose to criticize the "undue influence" of Gorbachev's wife, Raisa! The government decided to halt live coverage of the proceedings of the Congress when supervisors in many places complained that no work was being done because the workers were busy watching the latest arguments in Moscow.

The agenda at the early sessions of the Congress was limited to only two major items. The delegates were to select a chairperson for the legislature who would act, in effect, as Soviet president. Then they were to choose 542 of their members as representatives to a smaller legislative body, the Supreme Soviet, which would serve as the country's permanent legislature.

It was widely assumed that the overwhelming choice for the presidency would be Mikhail Gorbachev. A group of opposition legislators attempted to nominate Boris Yeltsin, but Yeltsin withdrew, knowing that at this time he would have no chance of defeating Gorbachev. In the end, Gorbachev ran unopposed and received 96 percent of the votes cast.

The Communist-dominated majority in the Congress also overwhelmed the liberal opposition when the members of the permanent Supreme Soviet were selected. So complete was the pro government sweep that at first even Yeltsin, by far the best known and most popular of the opposition deputies, did not gain a seat in the permanent legislature. Yeltsin's exclusion was greeted by cries of protest from the opposition delegates. One opposition delegate rose to denounce the "Stalinist-Brezhnevite Supreme Soviet" that had been created.

Within hours, thousands of everyday citizens were rallying in front of Moscow's huge Palace of the Congresses, demanding that Yeltsin be seated. In a display of public opinion never before seen in Soviet history, thousands of men and women across the nation telephoned their delegates in Moscow or sent telegrams asking that Yeltsin be included on the final list of members of the Supreme Soviet.

At the next morning's session, Aleksei Kazannik, a law professor from Siberia, rose to state that he would forfeit the seat he had gained in the Supreme Soviet if the Congress would agree to give the seat to Yeltsin instead. The Communist deputies realized that in attempting to exclude Yeltsin they had gone too far. Without a word of dissent, Kazannik's seat was given to Yeltsin.

That afternoon, as the Congress of People's Deputies completed its work for the day, another crowd gathered in front of the Palace of the Congresses. But unlike the anger that had marked the gathering the previous evening, now the mood was one of celebration. "Yeltsin! Yeltsin!" they cried. And as their hero left the hall and turned the corner to walk home to his apartment on Gorky Street, hundreds of men and women and children in the crowd followed him, creating a joyous victory celebration in the streets of Moscow.

▼ ▲ ▼

Throughout the remainder of 1989, the crises within Soviet society grew more severe. Nowhere did the situation seem more critical than in the three Baltic republics of Lithuania, Latvia, and Estonia, where resentment over Russian domination still ran high. August 23, 1989, marked the fiftieth anniversary of the Moscow-Berlin pact that had allowed Stalin to annex the Baltics to the USSR. In the Baltics that day, over 1 million people joined hands

People in the Estonian capital of Tallinn demonstrate to protest Soviet control of the Baltic states.

to form a human chain that was about 400 miles long and that linked the capitals of the three republics. As fall came, discontent with Soviet rule spread. Soon even Communist Party members in the Baltics were speaking out in favor of independence. In December the central committee of the Lithuanian Communist Party challenged the Moscow hierarchy directly and renounced its ties to the Communist Party of the Soviet Union.

Beyond the borders of the USSR, the Soviet bloc was collapsing as well. In June 1989 the Polish Communist Party suffered an overwhelming defeat in Poland's first free elections in more than 40 years. A new government led by members of the Solidarity movement was formed—the first non-Communist government in Eastern Europe since the end of World War II. In Hungary, too, radical political and economic reforms had been instituted, and the governing Socialist Workers Party collapsed under the pressure. Then on November 9, 1989, the Communist government of East Germany announced the lifting of all restrictions on travel to the West, turning the once impregnable Berlin Wall into a meaningless symbol. That same week protests broke out in Bulgaria. By the end of the year, the Communist government there would be out of power as well. On November 19, hundreds of thousands of protesters filled the streets of Czechoslovakia's capital, Prague. Soon a nonviolent "velvet revolution" would sweep the Czechoslovak Communists from power. Finally, on Christmas Day 1989, Romania's Communist dictator, Nicolae Ceaușescu, was executed by a firing squad.

▼ ▲ ▼

In December 1989 the Congress of People's Deputies gathered in Moscow for its second session. Opposition delegates led by Andrei Sakharov were determined not to let Gorbachev dominate the proceedings. Time and again, Sakharov rose to denounce the government's policies or to demand some specific reform.

On December 12, Sakharov and Gorbachev had their final confrontation. Sakharov approached the podium of the Congress carrying a large cloth sack. In it, he said, were telegrams and petitions from 60,000 Soviet citizens. From all across the USSR, Sakharov said, men and women had written to him, demanding the repeal of Article Six of the Soviet constitution, which guaranteed the "leading role" of the Communist Party in the life of the nation. It was time for the Congress to eliminate the party's leading role, Sakharov urged, and establish the Soviet Union as a genuine multiparty democracy.

Gorbachev ordered Sakharov to take his seat. But Sakharov pushed on. "Sixty thousand signatures!" he exclaimed, just as his microphone went dead.[2] At Gorbachev's urging, the Communist majority, which still controlled the assembly, immediately defeated Sakharov's motion to repeal Article Six.

On the evening of December 14, Sakharov returned to his apartment after yet another long, heated session. He ate a light supper, worked in his study for several hours, and then went to bed. He told his wife, Elena Bonner, that he was tired and not feeling very well. By the next morning, Sakharov was dead of a heart attack. The Soviet Union had lost one of its most persistent voices of reform.

Hard-liners and reformers alike were shocked by the news. Several days later, Gorbachev himself stood as an honorary pallbearer beside Sakharov's casket. Later he delivered an emotional tribute to the man with whom he had disagreed so many times.

Sakharov was dead, but the cause to which the great scientist had dedicated the final years of his life was stronger than ever. Even Gorbachev realized that events like those that had taken place in Poland, Hungary, East Germany, Bulgaria, Czechoslovakia, and even Romania might soon take place in the Soviet Union unless more daring reforms

A confrontation took place between Gorbachev *(left)* and Sakharov at the second session of the Congress of People's Deputies in December 1989.

were made. In a relatively short time, many of the reforms Sakharov had proposed would become official policies of Gorbachev's government.

As the year 1989 gave way to a new decade and as the long Russian winter dragged on, Mikhail Gorbachev could be heard uttering words strikingly similar to those Sakharov had spoken in calling for the repeal of Article Six of the Soviet constitution. Communist domination should no longer be assumed, Gorbachev declared. The Communist Party must now earn the support of the Soviet people. No longer, he said, should Communists fear their own people in the way that "the devil is afraid of incense."[3]

But in spite of these bold words the country's economic situation continued to worsen. Throughout the summer and fall of 1989, coal miners across the country had been on strike. The lack of coal, combined with a severe decline in oil production, had led to a nationwide energy crisis. The crisis depressed production in many industries; agriculture was affected as well. While the nation's collective and state farms were able to harvest enough food to feed the people of the Soviet Union, the nation's system of distribution was near collapse. To stave off severe food shortages—perhaps even famine— the Soviet government had to import huge amounts of grain from the West. These imports, along with a decline in exports that accompanied the overall industrial decline (as well as shrinking demand for Soviet goods due to the collapse of the Soviet bloc in Eastern Europe), resulted in a massive trade imbalance that threatened to bankrupt the national treasury.

▼ ▲ ▼

Soon Soviet citizens followed their counterparts in Eastern Europe into the streets. On the morning of Sunday, February 4, 1990, over 200,000 citizens of Moscow gathered to demand an end to the Communist Party's monopoly on power. The message was not lost on Gorbachev. The next day at a meeting of the central committee, the general secretary proposed repealing Article Six. It was time to establish a multiparty system, Gorbachev said, a system that would reflect the party's new ideals of "humane, democratic socialism." Furthermore, the Communist Party needed to "cleanse itself of everything . . . linked with the authoritarian-bureaucratic system" of the past.[4]

If Gorbachev thought that his speech would satisfy Boris Yeltsin and other radicals in the party, he was wrong. Yeltsin believed that, once again, Gorbachev was trying to have it both ways. He spoke of the need for reforms but was not doing enough to bring them about. The general secretary's speech sounded as though "it was written with both hands: the right and the left," Yeltsin complained.[5]

But when a vote was finally taken, Yeltsin stood alone in voting not to accept Gorbachev's report. On February 7, 1990, the central committee eliminated the leading role of the Communist Party from the Soviet constitution.

▼ ▲ ▼

Over the next several weeks, long-scheduled elections for representatives to local soviets went ahead as planned. As in earlier elections for the Congress of People's Deputies, the results offered little good news to the Communist Party. In the Slavic heartland of the Soviet Union—the three republics of Russia, Byelorussia, and the Ukraine—leading Communist officials were decisively defeated. A nationalist slate swept the elections in the western Ukraine, and reformers gained majorities in the city governments of Moscow, Leningrad, and Minsk.

To the north in Lithuania, the nationalist organization Sajudis garnered 90 seats in the republic's Supreme Soviet. The Lithuanian Communist Party gained only 29. Nationalist fronts won similar victories in the other two Baltic republics.

Gorbachev sensed that the very existence of the Soviet Union was in danger. The month before, at his urging, the national Supreme Soviet had passed a law expanding his powers. Previously the chairmanship of the Soviet had been a largely ceremonial post. Under Gorbachev's proposals, however, the president would become the nation's chief executive officer, as well as the commander in chief of its armed forces.

The Supreme Soviet approved the idea of an expanded presidency by a vote of 306 to 65. The proposal next had to be acted on by the Congress of People's Deputies, where almost all 400 delegates of the Inter-Regional Group opposed Gorbachev's proposals. Nationalist representatives from the Baltic states, as well as from the Caucasus republics of Georgia, Azerbaijan, and Armenia, also felt that their sovereignty would be threatened by the imposition of a strong central presidency on the entire union.

Gorbachev realized that he would have difficulty gaining the two-thirds vote needed for passage of his proposals. To win over some opponents of the plan, Gorbachev agreed to certain limitations on the president's powers, including his right to declare a state of emergency in republics beyond Russia. In the end the expanded presidency was adopted, as were other important constitutional changes legalizing opposition political parties and allowing the private ownership of businesses and land.

On March 15, Gorbachev was elected president. Even though he ran without opposition, his margin of 1,329 for and 495 against was barely more than the two thirds needed for election. In addition to the 495 opposition delegates who voted against Gorbachev, another 420, mostly hard-line Communists, abstained from voting.

Almost immediately, Gorbachev's victory was overshadowed by news from the Baltics. A few days before the election, the Sajudis-dominated Supreme Soviet of Lithuania had declared that republic's independence and had severed all official connections to the central government in Moscow. A new flag and national anthem were adopted and all Soviet symbols in the legislature's meeting hall were removed. Vytautas Landsbergis, a scholarly musician with little political experience, was elected Lithuania's president. As one of its first acts, the new Lithuanian government demanded that the Soviet Union immediately withdraw all its troops from Lithuanian territory.

Gorbachev had no intention of recognizing Lithuania's independence. He denounced the legislature's declaration as "illegitimate and invalid" and demanded that it be rescinded at once. He would not even consider entering into negotiations with Sajudis. Rather than withdrawing Soviet troops from Lithuanian territory, Gorbachev ordered them on full alert and sent additional KGB troops to Vilnius, the Lithuanian capital. Lithuanian soldiers in the Soviet army were forbidden to leave their barracks, out of fear that they might desert.

Gradually, Gorbachev increased the pressure on the Lithuanians. He imposed an economic embargo on the republic and cut off its supplies of oil and natural gas. But the Lithuanians refused to back down. They responded to the Soviet embargo by cutting back fuel consumption. Soon, bicycles rather than cars filled the streets of Lithuania's cities. But in spite of such courage and determination, most observers believed that it would be only a matter of time before the Lithuanians were forced to capitulate to the Soviets.

▼ ▲ ▼

May Day, or International Workers' Day as it is known officially, was always marked in the USSR by a huge parade through Moscow's Red Square. Tradition held that party and government leaders should preside over this display of Soviet strength and power from a special viewing platform high atop Lenin's mausoleum.

So it was that on May 1, 1990, Gorbachev climbed to the

top of the large red stone tomb in the center of Moscow. This year, however, the Communist Party leader was joined by several non-Communists as he reviewed the parade. Chief among these was Gavril Popov, Moscow's new mayor and a leader of the Inter-Regional Group. Since the death of Sakharov, Popov had emerged as one of the opposition's most outspoken leaders. At the insistence of Popov and the Moscow city council, the tightly organized May Day parades of past years had been replaced in 1990 by a free and open event in which all who wished to could participate.

It soon became obvious that May Day 1990 would be different in other respects as well. The official delegations at

Thousands of Muscovites parade through Red Square on May 1, 1990, denouncing Communist Party rule. The banner in the foreground reads, "Democracy, Perestroika, Glasnost."

the front of the parade were followed by a swelling mass of regular Soviet citizens. Some carried banners and posters. Others had large portraits of Sakharov and Yeltsin. Still others shouted slogans and shook their fists as they passed before their leaders on the platform.

"Down with the Cult of Lenin!" read one of the banners. "Marxism-Leninism Is on the Rubbish Heap of History," read another. Other banners suggested that the Communist leadership should move to Chernobyl. One protester likened Gorbachev to Nicolae Ceauşescu, the Romanian dictator who had been executed a few months earlier.

Gorbachev withstood this unprecedented, unrestrained outpouring of his citizens' anger for a half hour. Finally, however, he had had enough. He turned and stormed off the podium, followed closely by the other members of the Communist leadership. The next day a scathing editorial appeared in the official newspaper *Izvestia*, scolding the demonstrators for their rudeness. Another *Izvestia* commentator mused that "some people want to burst out angrily at Gorbachev with . . . everything that our grandfathers, fathers, and, of course, we ourselves did not dare to say to Stalin, Khrushchev, and Brezhnev."[6] Within two weeks of the May Day demonstrations, the Supreme Soviet passed a new law threatening a prison term of up to six years for anyone who dared to "slander" the president of the USSR.

Meanwhile, the government of Prime Minister Nikolai Ryzhkov struggled to implement its program of economic reform. While many praised the ultimate goal of Ryzhkov's plan—establishment of a "regulated market economy" within the socialist system of the USSR—there was little support for the particular programs that the prime minister proposed. Central to Ryzhkov's proposals were price increases on many consumer goods. The price of bread, for example, was scheduled to triple within a few months. While Ryzhkov promised that workers' wages would increase as well, he gave no indication as to where the government would find the funds needed to pay these increased salaries.

When word of the proposed price increases leaked out, panic-buying swept the nation. Within a few days, no bread was left on bakery shelves; a little later, supplies of flour and pasta ran out as well. Gorbachev called for calm and restraint, but it seemed as though people had stopped listening to him. Many were now looking toward other political leaders to guide their nation through troubled times.

chapter 8

Out of Control

On May 29, 1990, the Supreme Soviet of the Russian Federation elected Boris Yeltsin as its chairman. Yeltsin was now, in effect, the president of Russia. He wasted no time in taking advantage of his new position. At Yeltsin's urging, Russia's legislature passed an act declaring its sovereignty, or independent status, within the USSR. Henceforth, laws of the Russian Federation would take precedence over those of the Soviet Union.

In spite of the fact that his chief opponent was now president of the largest Soviet republic, Gorbachev tried to put a good face on the situation. He declared that he and Yeltsin shared "common goals and tasks" and that he looked forward to working with Yeltsin and the Russian parliament in a "normal, businesslike" manner.[1] Gorbachev also proposed convening a new federation council, composed of the leaders of all 15 republics in the Soviet Union.

But soon, events seemed to spin out of Gorbachev's control. In July 1990 the Soviet Communist Party held its Twenty-eighth Congress in Moscow. It quickly became obvious just how badly divided the party was. First, Yegor Ligachev made a speech blaming Gorbachev and his reform-minded followers for the decline of Soviet influence in Eastern Europe. Then it was the turn of Yeltsin and the radicals. The past errors of the Communist Party had "discredited those Communists who are sincere and consistent supporters of change," Yeltsin charged.[2] But while hard-line conservatives were deeply entrenched in the party apparatus, Yeltsin said, in society at large, the people were demanding genuine democracy and change. If the party refused to remake itself radically, Yeltsin concluded, then the people would follow the lead of people elsewhere in Eastern Europe and sweep Communism aside.

Yeltsin had already make up his mind about his future as a Communist. On July 12, in a speech before the party congress, he announced his resignation from the party. As long as he remained under the discipline of the Communist Party, Yeltsin said, he would not be able to serve as a fair, evenhanded president of all of the people of Russia. Then, with his speech completed, Yeltsin dramatically strode down the center aisle of the large hall and out the door.

▼ ▲ ▼

Now Yeltsin turned his full attention to governing the immense Russian Federation. For months, he had been pressing Gorbachev to support the economic proposals of his chief economic advisor, Stanislav Shatalin. Under the Shatalin plan, large state-controlled enterprises were to be dismantled, and a free-market economy was to be established in the USSR within 500 days. But Gorbachev hesitated. He feared that accepting such radical proposals—including permitting the ownership of private property—would leave him open to charges that he was abandoning socialism.

Aides of Boris Yeltsin applaud the announcement of his election as president of the Russian Federation.

Throughout the summer of 1990, the country's economic situation worsened. When bread supplies in Moscow again ran out, thousands took to the streets in protest. By fall, Gorbachev had lost faith in Prime Minister Ryzhkov's more moderate economic plan, and with Yeltsin at his side he announced his acceptance of Shatalin's "500 Days" plan.

In October 1990 the Nobel Foundation in Sweden announced that it had awarded the 1990 Nobel Peace Prize to Mikhail Gorbachev. But Gorbachev could take scant comfort in the award. While he was still a highly respected world leader, his popularity within the USSR was at an all-time low. By the autumn of 1990, according to public opinion polls, fewer than 20 percent of Soviet citizens supported Gorbachev's policies.

Gorbachev himself often seemed uncertain as to what his next step should be. Sometimes he spoke of conciliation and cooperation with Yeltsin and the radicals, while at other times he seemed to be calling for a return to the more rigid ways of the past. In mid-October, proponents of radical economic reform were bitterly disappointed when Gorbachev backed away from his support of the Shatalin plan and unveiled his own slower approach to economic reform. While in the past he had spoken of the need for the central government to share power with the republics, in November, at Gorbachev's urging, the Supreme Soviet declared that the separate republics had no right to assert the primacy of their own laws over those of the national government—a step that the legislatures of all 15 Soviet republics had already taken. As if to thumb their noses at the Supreme Soviet's declaration, the legislatures of the two largest republics, Russia and the Ukraine, immediately passed resolutions reaffirming the primacy of their own laws.

Late in November, Gorbachev sent the leaders of the republics a proposal for a new union treaty, governing relationships among the 15 Soviet republics. Under this proposal, the laws of the central government in Moscow would still take precedence over those of the separate republics, but the republics were granted the right to determine their own forms of government and economic structures. Even the name of the country was to be changed—to the Union of Soviet *Sovereign* Republics.

Although some republican leaders greeted Gorbachev's proposal with cautious hope, others were not impressed.

Boris Yeltsin agreed that Gorbachev's proposals did not go far enough.

▼ ▲ ▼

Throughout the winter of 1990, life in the USSR grew increasingly grim. There were widespread shortages of the most basic necessities, and for the first time since World War II there was fear that many Soviet citizens might face starvation. The Soviet government appealed for assistance from foreign governments and charities. Gorbachev himself signed an open letter in the German magazine *Stern*, asking Germany to send 500,000 tons of meat, 500,000 tons of vegetable oil, and 100,000 tons of noodles to ward off famine in the Soviet Union. The country seemed on the verge of economic collapse.

Gorbachev responded by moving toward a more hard-line position. On November 27 the minister of defense, Dmitri Yazov, appeared on national television. In a stern voice he read a series of presidential decrees authorizing the army to respond to attacks by civilians with deadly force if necessary. On December 2 the interior minister, Vadim Bakatin, one of the chief reformers in Gorbachev's government, was fired. His replacement was Boris Pugo, a dedicated Communist and former head of the Latvian KGB. Pugo's chief assistant was to be Boris Gromov, an army general who had emerged as one of the Congress of People's Deputies' chief critics of *perestroika*. Many wondered why Gorbachev was allowing himself to be surrounded by so many of his former political enemies. When the head of the KGB, Vladimir Kryuchkov, appeared on national television a few days later and spoke of the need to suppress "anti-Communist" elements within

Shevardnadze announces his resignation to the Congress of People's Deputies.

the USSR "with all means at [our] disposal,"[3] many feared that Gorbachev was being pushed aside by conservatives inside his own government.

On December 20, 1990, Foreign Minister Eduard Shevardnadze appeared before a session of the Congress of People's Deputies. "A dictatorship is coming," Shevardnadze told a shocked audience. He continued, "As a man, as a citizen, as a Communist, I can not reconcile myself with what is happening in my country and to the trials which await our people." No longer could he cooperate with "boys in colonels' epaulets" who seemed destined to take over the country's government. Therefore, Shevardnadze concluded, he had no choice but to resign.[4] With that, Shevardnadze stepped down from the podium and left the Kremlin's Palace of the Congresses.

Gorbachev, sitting at Shevardnadze's side during the

speech, seemed completely overcome by his foreign minister's words. He too left the hall quickly. When he regained his composure enough to address the delegates two hours later, he reported that Shevardnadze would not reconsider his decision to resign, nor would he recant his declaration that the country stood on the verge of a dictatorship. Shevardnadze had done much good for the cause of *perestroika*, Gorbachev continued, but to resign at such an important juncture in the country's history, and without consulting anyone—not even Gorbachev, the president—was "unforgivable," Gorbachev said.

Gorbachev also claimed that he had been planning to appoint Shevardnadze as his vice president. Instead, a few days later Gorbachev announced his nomination of Gennadi Yanayev for the position. To many, Gorbachev's choice seemed especially uninspired. Yanayev had gradually worked his way up through the ranks of the party and had been appointed to the Politburo just a few months before. In earlier years Yanayev had been seen as a staunch Gorbachev loyalist, a firm supporter of perestroika. But in recent months, he had moved closer to the conservatives. "I am a Communist to the depths of my soul," Yanayev declared as he accepted the nomination.[5]

Yegor Ligachev, longtime head of the conservative faction within the party, declared that Gorbachev had made a "great choice" in selecting Yanayev as his vice president. Reformers, however, felt betrayed by Gorbachev's choice. Once again, it seemed that the president was giving in to the hard-liners. Indeed, so many delegates were unenthusiastic about Yanayev that on the first ballot he failed to secure the majority of votes needed for election in spite of the fact that he was the only candidate standing for the office. Only an emotional speech from Gorbachev convinced enough delegates to support Yanayev on the second ballot to secure his election by the slimmest of margins.

▼ ▲ ▼

Soon, many began to see signs that Shevardnadze had been right in predicting the emergence of a dictatorship. On January 2, 1991, a special unit of Soviet security troops seized control of the largest newspaper in the Lithuanian capital of Vilnius. Five days later, on January 7, the ministry of defense announced that it was sending troops to the seven most troublesome republics (Armenia, Estonia, Georgia, Latvia, Lithuania, Moldavia, and the western Ukraine) to enforce the military draft and round up deserting soldiers.

Afraid that a major crackdown was about to take place, the prime minister of Lithuania, Kazimiera Prunskiene, hurried to Moscow on January 8. She appealed to Gorbachev not to use force, and instead to open negotiations to settle the differences between the Lithuanian government and the Soviet authorities. According to Prunskiene, Gorbachev greeted her coldly and told her to "go back home and restore order." Otherwise, the Soviet leader said, he would have to do so himself. Prunskiene asked if she could assure the people of Lithuania that force would not be used by the Soviets. "You cannot give them any assurances that I have not given you" was all that Gorbachev would say.[6]

Two days later, Gorbachev sent a message to the Lithuanian government, accusing it of "flagrant violations and deviations from the USSR constitution" and of attempting to restore an anti-Communist government.

Early the next morning, hundreds of specially trained paratroopers landed in the center of Vilnius and took control of the capital's airport and railroad station. A "national salvation committee" headed by members of a pro-Moscow faction within the Lithuanian Communist Party declared itself Lithuania's new government.

The next morning—Sunday, January 13—a column of Soviet tanks rolled through the streets of Vilnius to the national television tower. When a group of about 30 men and women tried to block the way, a tank rolled right over them. Many were seriously injured, and at least one person was killed. When the defenders of the tower still refused to disperse, a heavily armed squadron of paratroopers turned on them with clubs and rifle butts. By the end of the day, at least 14 Lithuanian civilians had been killed.

That evening, Boris Pugo, the Soviet interior minister, appeared on national television. He blamed the violence in Vilnius on Lithuanian nationalists, who had attacked the Soviet troops "with real bayonets."[7] Pugo added that the Lithuanian people themselves had appealed to Moscow for assistance—a statement with absolutely no basis in fact.

Gorbachev had remained silent throughout the entire crackdown in Vilnius. Finally, on January 14 he told reporters that he had known nothing about the violence at the television tower until it was over—"when they woke me up," Gorbachev said. "We didn't want this to happen," Gorbachev continued, but he refused to speak out against the attack or those who had ordered it. Instead, he too condemned the Lithuanian nationalists. They had created the unfortunate situation, Gorbachev said, by continuing to press their unreasonable demands.[8]

If Gorbachev would not speak out against the violence in Vilnius, hundreds of thousands of other Soviet citizens

106 The Soviet Turmoil

Lithuanians shout at a Soviet Army tank that took part in the takeover of the national TV tower.

would. Soon, city streets across the country were filled with large crowds protesting Lithuania's "Bloody Sunday." In Moscow, one banner declared, "Down With Gorbachev the Bloody One!" Another likened Gorbachev to Saddam Hussein, the Iraqi dictator who had invaded Kuwait. Boris Yeltsin immediately declared his support for the people of the Baltics, and the Russian government entered into agreements with the three Baltic nations. Yeltsin even flew to the Latvian capital, Riga, where a crackdown was also feared.

▼ ▲ ▼

Throughout that crisis-filled winter, Gorbachev seemed like a man caught in the middle. In March he created a new security council to help him govern the country. Conservative hard-liners, including Yanayev, Pugo, and Kryuchkov, assumed the most prominent posts. But Gorbachev never established the presidential dictatorship that many predicted would be his next step. To the contrary, he continued to speak of his desire for further democratization. "I wanted to gain time by making tactical moves," Gorbachev later wrote of his relationship with the hard-liners. "I had to outmaneuver them."[9] But to others, Gorbachev's often contradictory policies were nothing more than the desperate vacillations of a man no longer in control of the situation.

On March 17 the voters of the USSR went to the polls to decide the question "Do you consider it necessary to preserve the Union of Soviet Socialist Republics as a renewed federation of equal Soviet republics, in which the rights and freedoms of peoples of any nationality will be fully guaranteed?" Even though Yeltsin and many other reformers called the vote a meaningless exercise, more than 70 percent of those voting were in favor of preserving the USSR. (The referendum was not held in Latvia, Lithuania, Estonia, or Georgia.)

In spite of the outcome of the referendum, Yeltsin continued to assert Russian sovereignty. Early in March he had called upon Gorbachev to resign. A few days after the referendum he stepped up his rhetoric and called upon the people of Russia to "declare war upon the leadership of the country, which has led us into a quagmire."[10] Soon after, huge demonstrations in favor of Yeltsin were being held in cities across the country.

But on March 28 an emergency session of the Russian Congress of People's Deputies met to consider an article of impeachment against Yeltsin. The resolution had been offered by hard-line Communist deputies, who charged that in his speeches earlier in the month Yeltsin had called for open rebellion against the Soviet government. This, they said, was grounds for removing him from office.

Three days before, on March 25, the Soviet interior ministry had announced a ban on all demonstrations in the streets of Moscow. The ban was to stay in effect for three weeks—longer than the duration of the Russian Congress. In this way the Soviet government hoped to ward off any further demonstrations in support of Yeltsin.

But Yeltsin's supporters were not put off. Democratic Russia, the chief group supporting Yeltsin, announced a public demonstration for the same day as the opening of the emergency session. The day before, KGB chief Kryuchkov, Interior Minister Pugo, and Vice President Yanayev went to see Gorbachev. They told him they had information that pro-Yeltsin forces were planning to use ropes and climbing hooks to scale the walls of the Kremlin. Then they would storm the chief government offices and seize power. The hard-liners urged Gorbachev to mobilize 50,000 troops to turn back the demonstrations. Gorbachev reluctantly agreed.

The next morning, over 100,000 people marched through central Moscow toward the Kremlin. Immediately, troops were sent to block the march and order the demonstrators to return to their homes. But the crowd held its ground. A tense standoff continued for several hours. Finally, Gorbachev issued a statement announcing that he would pull back the troops, but only if the demonstrators left the streets voluntarily. When word of Gorbachev's compromise reached them, the protesters responded with a great shout of joy. Their demonstration had been held as planned, and violence had been averted. Gradually the demonstrators dispersed, shouting pro-Yeltsin slogans as they went. By early that night, Gorbachev kept his part of the deal and removed all troops from the streets of the capital.

▼ ▲ ▼

In compromising with the demonstrators, Gorbachev again seemed to veer away from the hard-liners and toward the forces of democracy and reform. While in public he continued to stress the need for a strong central government to deal with the wave of demonstrations and strikes that was sweeping the country, behind the scenes he was working feverishly to complete a new union treaty.

On April 23, Gorbachev and the leaders of nine of the Soviet republics met secretly in the town of Novo-Ogaryevo outside Moscow. After an intense all-day negotiating session, the participants in the so-called Nine Plus One talks agreed to take "urgent measures to stabilize the situation in the country and overcome the crisis."[11] All agreed to meet again in the near future to draft both a new union treaty and a new Soviet constitution.

The day after signing the agreement, Gorbachev returned to Moscow for a special meeting of the central committee. At this meeting one conservative critic after another denounced the general secretary. "Mikhail Sergeyevich, you have simply taken your hands off the wheel," one delegate scolded. "The whole government machine is effectively leaderless." A Ukrainian member spoke of the "mistakes, indecisiveness, and halfheartedness" of the entire government, especially the president.[12] Gorbachev must be decisive, do his duty, and establish order, the deputy insisted.

Finally, Gorbachev's patience was exhausted. Over the objections of the presiding officer, he demanded to be heard. He then delivered what one observer has called Gorbachev's shortest speech, less than one minute in duration.

> *Okay, that's enough, now I'll answer everyone. I have to admit that about 70 percent of those who have taken the floor have declared that the popularity and authority of the General Secretary have dropped to almost nil. I think that neither the man nor the Party can remain in such a situation. This would be criminal.*
>
> *I suggest that debate cease and that the problem of the General Secretary be dealt with—as well as who will take his place until the next Congress. Also, who will suit the two, three, or four parties in this hall.*
>
> *For my part I want to say that the interests of the Party and state are no less dear to me than*

they are to those who have appeared in the political arena in the last two weeks. I resign.[13]

With that, Gorbachev stormed out of the hall angrily. Confusion reigned. No one knew what to do next. During a recess in the proceedings, Gorbachev's supporters on the central committee gathered. Finally they decided to draw up a petition saying that they too would leave the party if Gorbachev was allowed to resign. As battered and tarnished as the general secretary's reputation was, Gorbachev remained to many Soviet Communists the linchpin holding their party together. While many conservatives would have been pleased to have Gorbachev out of the way, they were not willing to risk the divisiveness—perhaps even the disintegration of the entire party—that removing him might cause. When the central committee meeting reconvened, a motion to reject Gorbachev's resignation passed by a vote of 322 to 13, with 14 abstentions.

With the conservative challenge within the party averted, Gorbachev moved even closer to Yeltsin and the reformers. Throughout the spring of 1991, the two presidents worked out several joint agreements between the Russian Federation and the central government. They also began to appear together at important public events and even began saying complimentary things about one another on evening news broadcasts. When in June Gorbachev traveled to Norway to accept the 1990 Nobel Peace Prize, both the foreign and Soviet press praised him as a great reformer and daring political leader. It was almost like the early days of *glasnost* and *perestroika*, when "Gorbymania" had swept the nations of the West.

But since Gorbachev's coming to power in 1985, the USSR had undergone immense changes. While Gorbachev was in Oslo accepting the Nobel Prize, the Russian presidential campaign entered full swing. For the first time ever, the people of Russia were allowed to choose their leader in free elections. While Yeltsin was favored to win, he was by no means unopposed. One of his opponents was Nikolai Ryzhkov, the former Soviet prime minister, who was the choice of many who favored closer ties with the central government. Another candidate was Vladimir Zhirinovsky. Zhirinovsky was an extreme Russian nationalist who dreamed of restoring the past glory, and territory, of the former Russian empire. Zhirinovsky went so far as to propose that Russia reclaim its control over Poland, Finland, and even Alaska.

Yeltsin won an easy victory in the election on June 12. He had gained over 57 percent of the vote, compared with less than 18 percent for Ryzhkov, who finished second. Zhirinovsky's total was about 8 percent. Now Yeltsin could claim that he had been directly chosen by his own people in a free election—something that no other leader in the Soviet Union, including Gorbachev, could say.

▼ ▲ ▼

On June 17 the participants in the original Nine Plus One negotiations met again to initial a draft of the new treaty of union. A final treaty would be submitted to the legislatures of the republics by the end of the summer.

The conservative Communists around Gorbachev feared they would be the big losers under the terms of the Nine Plus One agreement. They had no intention of giving up 74 years of Communist power so readily. Leading conservatives, including the new Soviet premier, Valentin Pavlov, met secretly to discuss how the new treaty might be shelved. Finally a plan was developed. At a session of the

Supreme Soviet on June 17, Pavlov requested special emergency powers. He was asking for these new powers for Gorbachev's own good, he said. The general secretary was working too hard, and many things in the country had gotten out of hand. Therefore, some "details" of government—including control over the national economy, the armed forces, the police, and the KGB—should be transferred to the premier.

The next day several other leading conservatives spoke in favor of Pavlov's proposal. Defense Minister Dmitri Yazov claimed that the nation's armed forces were on the verge of collapse. Interior Minister Boris Pugo spoke of the rise of lawlessness. KGB chief Vladimir Kryuchkov claimed that he had evidence of a plot by the American CIA to infiltrate the Soviet government.

Finally, on June 21, Gorbachev himself addressed the Supreme Soviet. Pavlov's claims were muddled nonsense, the Soviet president declared. His health was fine, and he was managing the affairs of state quite well. Gorbachev defended his past record and stressed some of the far-reaching plans that lay ahead, including the ratification of the Nine Plus One agreement. Gorbachev's address seemed to reassure the assembled delegates. By a vote of 262 to 24, they tabled Pavlov's request for emergency powers. "The coup is over!" a smiling, laughing Gorbachev told reporters afterwards. Gorbachev refused to move against any of the conservatives who had attempted to launch a "paper coup" against him.

On July 10, Gorbachev attended the inauguration of Boris Yeltsin as president of Russia. "Great Russia is rising from its knees!" Yeltsin declared. He promised to work to build "a prosperous, democratic, peaceful, genuinely sovereign, law-abiding state."[14] Once again the forces of reform and democracy seemed in control.

But there were less encouraging signs as well. On July 23 the newspaper *Sovetskaya Rossiya* published a lengthy manifesto signed by General Boris Gromov, Pugo's chief deputy in the interior ministry, and by Valentin Varennikov, a deputy in the ministry of defense. In their manifesto, "A Word to the People," Gromov and Varennikov demanded to know "how is it that we have let people come to power who do not love their country, who kowtow to foreign patrons and seek advice and blessings abroad?" It was time, the hard-line generals said, for the people of the Soviet Union to "wake up, come to our senses, rise in defense of our country and say No to those who have invaded it and are destroying it."[15]

Gorbachev shrugged off the manifesto and continued to prepare for a visit from the U.S. president George Bush at the end of July. Following Bush's departure, Gorbachev met with the leaders of several republics to put the final touches on the draft of the new union treaty, which was to be signed in Moscow later in August. To Gorbachev, reaching agreement on the treaty of union was one of the crowning achievements of his time in office. "It was like conquering Everest," he said.[16]

His work on the treaty completed, Gorbachev left for vacation at this villa on Cape Foros in the Crimea. In his own words, he would return to "a different country" three weeks later.

chapter 9

The Coup

Gorbachev's summer vacation was drawing to a close. Soon after coming to power in 1985, Gorbachev had had a luxurious presidential villa built at Cape Foros in the Crimea. Some said that construction of the opulent estate had cost the equivalent of $20 million or more—an enormous sum. At Foros, Gorbachev and his family enjoyed every conceivable luxury. There were tennis courts and an indoor swimming pool. They could stroll along beautifully landscaped pathways through olive groves and fruit trees. An escalator had even been constructed to transport them from the main house down to their private beach on the Black Sea. State-of-the-art security and communications systems had also been installed to guarantee Gorbachev's safety.

While Gorbachev had gone to Foros chiefly to rest, he had spent a few hours each day involved with affairs of state. On August 18, the last full day of his vacation, he had spent a busy day on the telephone with various officials throughout the USSR. Sometime after lunch, Vice President Yanayev called. He needed to know when Gorbachev's jet would be arriving in Moscow the next day so that he could meet the president at the airport.

After speaking with Yanayev, Gorbachev made a few more revisions to the speech he would deliver in Moscow on August 20 at the signing ceremony for the new union treaty. At just before 4:30 in the afternoon, he telephoned an assistant to discuss the revised draft. Gorbachev had been off the telephone only a few minutes, when at about 4:50, the head of his security detachment announced that visitors had arrived, demanding to see Gorbachev.

This was strange, Gorbachev thought. He had no other appointments scheduled and had planned to spend the rest of the afternoon and the evening with his family. The guard agreed that he had known nothing about the arrival of guests either.

"Then why did you let them in?" Gorbachev demanded.

"Plekhanov arrived with them," the guard replied. Yuri Plekhanov was the head of the Ninth Directorate of the KGB, which was charged with the security of high-ranking Soviet officials. Gorbachev picked up the telephone. It was dead, as were the four other telephones on his desk. Gorbachev realized that something was terribly wrong. Immediately he summoned his family to his study. "You must know that I will not give in to any kind of blackmail, nor to any threats or pressure," he told his wife, Raisa; his daughter, Irena; and her husband, Anatoly. He warned them that "anything could follow this"—arrest, imprisonment, even execution. Steadfastly they agreed to stand by Gorbachev "to the end, whatever was ahead."[1]

When his family left, the uninvited visitors entered. Gorbachev was shocked to see several of his closest advisors, including Valeri Boldin, his own chief of staff. Also in the group were Oleg Shenin, a member of the Politburo with whom Gorbachev had just spoken by telephone that morning; Oleg Baklanov, Gorbachev's chief advisor on the

Soviet Defense Council; Valentin Varennikov, a ranking general in the Soviet army; and, finally, KGB security chief Plekhanov.

"Who sent you?" Gorbachev immediately demanded to know.

"The committee," a member of the delegation replied.

"What committee?"

"The committee set up to deal with the emergency situation in the country."[2]

Gorbachev was flabbergasted. He had set up no such committee, he declared, nor had the Supreme Soviet.

The committee had assembled, one of the visitors said, and now demanded that Gorbachev either issue a decree declaring a state of emergency or hand over the power to Vice President Yanayev. Another visitor insisted that the country was headed toward a catastrophe and that drastic measures had to be taken.

Gorbachev angrily responded that he knew the situation in the country better than anyone. The dictatorial methods of the past must be rejected once and for all, he went on. Why not bring the issues up before a session of the Supreme Soviet instead and let the deputies decide what course of action to take next?

When the men before him seemed unmoved by his attempts at reason, Gorbachev berated them. "You and the people who sent you are irresponsible," he fumed. "You will destroy yourselves, but that's your business and to hell with you. But you will also destroy the country and everything we have already done. Tell that to the committee that sent you."[3]

But Gorbachev's opponents continued to insist that he resign or at least turn over power to Yanayev for the time being. Gorbachev steadfastly rejected their ultimatum, then continued to scold them.

"So tomorrow you will declare a state of emergency. What then? Can you plan for at least one day ahead, four steps further—what next? The country will reject these measures, it will not support them. . . . The people are not a battalion of soldiers to whom you can issue the command, 'Right turn' or 'Left turn, march,' and they will do as you tell them. It won't be like that. Just mark my words."[4]

The hard-liners then left Gorbachev alone in his office and completed the arrangements for cutting off Foros from the outside world. A division of troops was moved in to surround the town. Several ships were dispatched to cut off access from the sea. At about 7:30 P.M., with their work completed, the delegation returned to Moscow. Gorbachev was protected only by 32 men of his bodyguard, who had vowed to stand by their chief to the end.

▼ ▲ ▼

The coup against Gorbachev had been planned a few days after the Soviet president had left for vacation. On August 6, Kryuchkov had ordered two of his aides to write a detailed report on the situation in the country and the need for instituting a state of emergency. Soon Pavel Grachev from the ministry of defense joined in their discussions. All agreed that instituting a state of emergency at any time would be difficult—but after the signing of the new union treaty it would be impossible. At Kryuchkov's insistence, his aides and Grachev began making preparations for a move against Gorbachev. By August 16 the draft of the first statement of a planned "State Committee for the State of Emergency" (which would become known by its Russian abbreviation, GKChP) was ready, and

Kryuchkov ordered another of his deputies, Genii Ageyev, to travel to Foros to plan the disconnection of Gorbachev's communications system.

The next day, August 17, Kryuchkov called a meeting of several of the men who would make up the emergency committee. Present were Defense Minister Yazov, Prime Minister Pavlov, Politburo member Shenin, Gorbachev's chief of staff Boldin, and Oleg Baklanov, chief of military industries.

The conspirators agreed that a state of emergency must be declared—with or without Gorbachev's support. Other leading hard-liners, including Vice President Gennadi Yanayev, Interior Minister Boris Pugo, and Anatoly Lukyanov, chairman of the Supreme Soviet, were notified of the impending coup.

▼ ▲ ▼

Late on August 18, Plekhanov reported on his meeting with Gorbachev in Foros. Gorbachev was too ill to continue with the duties of president, Plekhanov lied. He had suffered "a heart attack or stroke or something" and must be replaced at once.[5] It was up to Vice President Yanayev to sign the official declaration of the state of emergency, which would establish the GKChP and name Yanayev the acting president of the USSR.

But Yanayev hesitated. He was not qualified to be president, he said. He wanted to speak with Gorbachev personally before making such an important decision. But the other conspirators insisted. They repeated the lie that Gorbachev was ill. When he had recuperated and the situation in the country had been stabilized, he would again assume the Soviet presidency. Finally, after further cajoling from Kryuchkov and the others, Yanayev agreed to sign the declaration, as did all the others at the table.

The next morning the people of the USSR awoke to find that a hard-line coup d'état had taken control of their government. A dejected newscaster nervously read the text of an official statement from the GKChP.

> *We are addressing you at a grave, critical hour for the future of our Motherland and our peoples. A mortal danger has come to loom large over our great Motherland.*
>
> *The policy of reforms, launched at Mikhail Gorbachev's initiative and designed as a means to ensure the country's dynamic development and the democratization of social life, has entered for several reasons into a blind alley. . . .*
>
> *The country is sinking into a quagmire of violence and lawlessness.*
>
> *Never before in national history has the propaganda of sex and violence assumed such a scale, threatening the health and lives of future generations. Millions of people are demanding measures against the octopus of crime and glaring immorality.*[6]

Because of this "mortal danger" facing the USSR, the declaration concluded, a six-month-long state of emergency had to be declared.

Russian president Boris Yeltsin awoke to the news of the coup when his daughter Tanya rushed into his bedroom shouting, "Papa, get up! There's a coup!"

Yeltsin was exhausted. He had returned late the night before from Alma-Ata, where he had been meeting with Kazakh president Nursyltan Nazarbayev. "That's illegal!"

he shouted as he heard the news.[7] Quickly he called an emergency meeting. Soon, leading members of the Russian government gathered in the living room of Yeltsin's country home outside Moscow. At once they began composing an appeal to the people of Russia. Ruslan Khasbulatov, the speaker of the Russian parliament, served as secretary and copied down text dictated to him by Yeltsin and the others. When the appeal was completed, Yeltsin's daughters typed it and prepared it for publication.

The instigators of the coup had not bothered to isolate Yeltsin or any other opposition leaders. They had even neglected to cut the telephone and fax lines to Yeltsin's home in Arkhangelskoye. Soon the Russian leadership's appeal for resistance was being sent by fax to correspondents in Moscow, throughout the Russian Republic, and around the world.

By nine o'clock that morning, Yeltsin had decided to establish a command center at the Russian parliament building, known as the White House, in central Moscow. Yeltsin understood the danger of traveling into the capital. At the urging of his wife, Naina, he put a heavy bulletproof vest under his business suit. Several of the Russian president's advisors tried to dissuade him from driving directly into the city. Yeltsin briefly entertained a plan to disguise himself as a fisherman and travel up the Moscow River and into the capital by boat. Finally he decided just to take his chances and drive directly to the White House.

Unknown to Yeltsin and his supporters, their every move was being monitored by the Soviet army. The elite Alpha Division had been dispatched to Archangelskoye the night before. But while the plotters had dispatched the division to the woods behind Yeltsin's home, they had never issued precise orders that Yeltsin should be arrested. Thus the way for the Russian president to proceed to the capital was clear, in spite of the fact that he was being watched by an army division less than 100 yards away. At ten o'clock in the morning on August 19, orders for Yeltsin's arrest were finally issued. By that time, however, the Russian president had already arrived in Moscow.

Inside a heavily armed bunker in the basement of the White House, the leaders of the Russian government began organizing opposition to the coup. Parliament chair Khasbulatov and Russian vice president Alexander Rutskoi read the government's appeal, "To the Citizens of Russia," over a makeshift radio station. Khasbulatov and Ruskoi also called upon the people of Moscow to come and defend the White House and the legally elected government of Russia.

By midmorning the tanks and troops outside the Moscow city hall were surrounded by thousands of protesting citizens. At the headquarters of the Russian parliament, young students openly read the decree of Yeltsin and the Russian government in loud, defiant voices. Some brought the soldiers food and gifts; others tried to place bouquets of flowers in the barrels of the troops' guns. At noon the protesters in front of the White House were joined by Yeltsin himself. Courageously the Russian president walked down the front stairs of the Russian parliament building and then climbed onto a tank parked in front of the building, from which he planned to address the crowd.

"Citizens of Russia," Yeltsin began, "the legally elected president of the country has been removed from power. . . . We are dealing with a right-wing, reactionary, anti-constitutional coup d'etát."[8] All decrees of the GKChP were illegal, Yeltsin declared. It was the duty of all Russian citizens to resist the coup with all means at their disposal, including "a universal, unlimited" general strike.

Yeltsin was followed on the tank by Konstantin Kobets, Russia's defense minister. Soviet armed forces on Russian territory were now under the direct command of the Russian, and not the Soviet, government, Kobets declared. "Not a hand will be raised against the people or the duly elected president of Russia," he concluded.

Soon, crowds throughout the Russian capital were confronting armed troops as they sat in their tanks. "Don't shoot your own people!" some demanded. Others begged the soldiers to put down their weapons and go home. There were reports that some soldiers were following the people's advice. Others remained at their posts but

Boris Yeltsin addresses a crowd from atop a tank outside the Russian White House, urging them to resist the coup.

unloaded all live ammunition from their guns. At the Russian parliament building, Civil Defense Unit 34 became the first garrison officially to side with the opposition. Likewise, the military commanders in Russia's second largest city, Leningrad, gave in to the demands of the city's reformist mayor, Anatoly Sobchak, and announced that they would enforce the dictates of the emergency committee.

▼ ▲ ▼

Meanwhile in the Crimea, Gorbachev struggled to obtain accurate information about the situation. Late in the afternoon of August 19, he and his family watched the press conference of the emergency committee on television. Not even the Soviet government reporters present seemed to believe the hard-liners' tales about Gorbachev's mysterious "illness." Still, there was no way to know how the rest of the country was reacting to the coup. Surely, Gorbachev mused, there must be a way to let the Soviet people know the truth about what was happening. Finally, with the help of his son-in-law, Anatoly, Gorbachev videotaped a statement. Looking tired and pale, dressed in a simple cardigan sweater, Gorbachev declared that all reports that he was ill were complete lies. He appealed to his people to unmask the "crude deception" that was being carried out by the perpetrators of the coup.

Gorbachev recorded his statement four times. He also drafted a written statement. To this was added a note from the president's doctor testifying to Gorbachev's good health. While Gorbachev struggled to devise some way to smuggle these statements out of Foros, members of his bodyguard arrived with some encouraging news. Two security guards had found several shortwave radios in the kitchen, on which they were able to pick up foreign radio stations. "The best reception was from the BBC [British Broadcasting Corporation] and Radio Liberty," Gorbachev later wrote.[9] Soon Gorbachev would hear that the coup, barely a day old, was already showing signs of unravelling.

Yeltsin and his supporters seemed more in control with each passing hour. Technicians at the state television station dared to show news footage of Yelstin atop the tank on the nightly newsbroadcast. The defiant Russian president seemed especially heroic in comparison with the sad showing the coup leaders had made at their news conference that same day. Acting president Yanayev sounded almost hysterical, in spite of his protestations that affairs in the country were returning to normal. The camera seemed to focus on Yanayev's trembling hands, as well as the incredulous expressions on the faces of the reporters present as they listened again to tales of Gorbachev's "illness."

Nevertheless, the hard-liners still had vast military resources at their disposal, and the opposition feared that a massive assault on the White House might come at any time. Late in the afternoon of August 20, Yeltsin cut short a telephone conversation with British prime minister John Major when he received a report that Soviet army tanks were on their way to storm the parliament building.

While the reports of an imminent attack were incorrect, the coup's military command was meeting at that very hour to draft a plan of action. Over the prior two days, the hard-liners had moved thousands of troops into the capital. All main thoroughfares and public squares were surrounded by tanks. There had been sporadic reports of gunfire between Soviet troops and prodemocracy demonstrators, and three protesters had been killed when they were run over by a tank near the Garden Ring Road. There were also reports that the Alpha Group of the Soviet army, the same unit that had toppled the government of Afghanistan in a pro-Soviet coup in 1979, had been moved into place near the White House.

According to the military command's plan, Operation Thunder, Alpha Group would attack the parliament building with tanks and grenade launchers. Then a specially equipped team of commandos would be dispatched to the fifth floor of the building, where Yeltsin's office was located. There, these commandos would arrest Yeltsin, if possible. If he put up a struggle, he was to be killed. While Alpha Group forced its way into the White House, a second special unit, Beta Group, would put down any resistance outside the building. Additional KGB units would then be sent in to arrest other opposition leaders and secure the premises.

But while several leading hard-liners, most notably KGB director Kryuchkov, favored the rapid implementation of Operation Thunder, other command leaders hesitated. General Pavel Grachev, head of the Soviet air force and one of the earliest advocates of the state of emergency, now counseled delay and a negotiated settlement. General Lebed also recommended caution. "There is a huge crowd," Lebed told Deputy Defense Minister Vladislav Achalov at a Kremlin meeting on August 20. "They are building barricades. There will be heavy casualties. There are many armed men at the White House." Others added that, in their opinions, there was not sufficient force available to carry out Operation Thunder successfully. "We can't lose the initiative," Defense Minister Yazov responded angrily.[10] More troops would have to be called in. But Yazov's orders for reinforcements were never carried out.

Even within Alpha Group itself there was growing opposition to the coup. Anatoly Salayev, one of the unit's leaders, had already announced that he would not storm the parliament. "They want to smear us in blood," Salayev told his men.[11] By the end of the day, several other leading Soviet military leaders, including commanders Lebed and Grachev, would come over to the side of Yeltsin and the democrats.

At eight o'clock that evening, acting president Yanayev, appearing more disoriented with each passing hour, convened a meeting of the emergency committee. He began by saying that he had heard disturbing rumors that an attack on the White House was being planned by the military command. (Apparently the acting president had not been informed of plans to use force against opponents of the coup.) Perhaps the GKChP should issue an official statement assuring the public that the "rumors" were false, Yanayev suggested. Yanayev's comments were greeted with incredulous silence. Finally the confused Yanayev asked his colleagues, "Is there really someone here among us who wants to storm the White House?"[12]

Kryuchkov began to speak of the massive support the coup was receiving across the USSR, but Yanayev cut him short. One after another, the leaders of the republics were coming out in opposition to the coup, he said. There were reports of dissension within the army and even within the KGB. There were not enough troops loyal to the hardliners. There was not even enough food on hand to feed those who remained loyal. He had received telegrams, Yanayev said, hundreds of them, all expressing disapproval of Gorbachev's ouster. Perhaps the state of emergency had not been such a good idea after all.

In the early hours of the morning of August 21, Kryuchkov telephoned Gennadi Burbulis, one of Yeltsin's chief assistants at the White House. "You can go to sleep," Kryuchkov told Burbulis.[13] There would be no attack. The coup had just about breathed its last.

▼ ▲ ▼

By the morning of August 21, it was over. A few members of the emergency committee still held out for arresting Yeltsin. But few entertained any fantasies that the coup might be revived. Some of the members of the GKChP had left the committee entirely and had gone into hiding. Prime Minister Pavlov was reported to be in the hospital, suffering from exhaustion. Interior Minister Boris Pugo had returned to his apartment in Moscow the night before, deeply depressed. The next day, police would find him dead. Pugo shot himself in the head rather than face the reckoning that would follow the coup. The few hard-liners still occupying government offices in the Kremlin scrambled to dismantle the emergency committee and rescind the state of emergency.

At eight o'clock in the morning on August 21, Yazov met with his chief advisors. They all agreed that further action was useless. Yazov issued orders for all troops to return to their barracks and for the barricades around Moscow to be taken down. By the middle of the afternoon, the main roads in the Soviet capital were clogged with long lines of tanks heading out of the city. Tank drivers waved happily to cheering bystanders as both sides shouted together, "It's over!"

At about midday, Yeltsin addressed a special session of the Russian Supreme Soviet. He had just spoken with

Kryuchkov by telephone, the Russian president said, and they had both agreed to fly to the Crimea and bring Gorbachev back to Moscow. But many of Yeltsin's own supporters were suspicious. Suppose this was part of a plot by the hard-liners to draw Yeltsin out of the White House and arrest him. Instead the Russian government decided to send a delegation headed by Russian vice president Rutskoi and premier Ivan Silayev.

Immediately the hard-liners saw the need to get to Foros before the Russian delegation. Perhaps they believed that Gorbachev might still be willing to sign a declaration of a state of emergency, thus acknowledging the need for their actions of the past few days. There were yet fears that the hard-liners might try to take Gorbachev hostage or otherwise harm him. Apparently, when Raisa Gorbachev heard reports on the BBC that a delegation from the emergency committee was on its way to Foros "to show the Soviet people the state Gorbachev was in," she suffered some sort of stroke and temporarily lost the ability to speak.

Two airplanes carrying representatives from the emergency committee left Vnukovo Airport in Moscow at about two o'clock in the afternoon on August 21. Among those on board were Kryuchkov and Yazov as well as Anatoly Lukyanov, chairman of the Supreme Soviet of the USSR, and Vladimir Ivashko, deputy general secretary of the Soviet Communist Party. The airplane carrying Rutskoi, Silayev, and the Russian delegation left about three hours later. It seemed as though the hard-liners would get to Gorbachev first.

However, just before Kryuchkov's aircraft landed in the Crimea, Yeltsin's forces managed to reestablish telephone communication with the presidential estate at Foros.

Yeltsin warned Gorbachev not to meet with the members of the emergency committee "under any circumstances."

Gorbachev wasted no time in organizing his security detail. When Kryuchkov and Yazov arrived at the villa, they were immediately placed under house arrest. Gorbachev did agree to see Lukyanov, one of his closest personal friends since their college days at Moscow State University in the 1950s. When Lukyanov protested that he had had nothing to do with the coup, Gorbachev scolded him, "You've known me for forty years, Anatoly Ivanovich. "Don't hang noodles on my ears [the Russian expression for 'Don't make a fool of me']."[14]

Finally, at about 8:30 that evening, Rutskoi and the Russian delegation arrived. Gorbachev greeted them excitedly. "He was nearly trembling with excitement," Rutskoi said later.

Gorbachev's wife, Raisa, however, was more sullen. Later, Rutskoi would also describe her appearance: "You know how bright she normally looks, but when we saw her, she looked on the verge of a heart attack—I mean, completely shaken up. . . ."[15] When Gorbachev asked her if she felt well enough to fly back to Moscow that very evening, she did not hesitate. "Yes," she replied. "We must fly immediately."[16]

At the Belbek military airport a few miles from Foros, Gorbachev and his party had two airplanes to choose from for their trip back to the capital: the official presidential jet in which the members of the emergency committee had flown to the Crimea, and a smaller Aeroflot jet in which Rutskoi and the Russian delegation had traveled. Still leery of treachery, Raisa insisted that they fly with the Russians. Gorbachev agreed and he apologized to his personal pilot. A few hours later, the Soviet president and his family arrived back at Vnukovo Airport near Moscow.

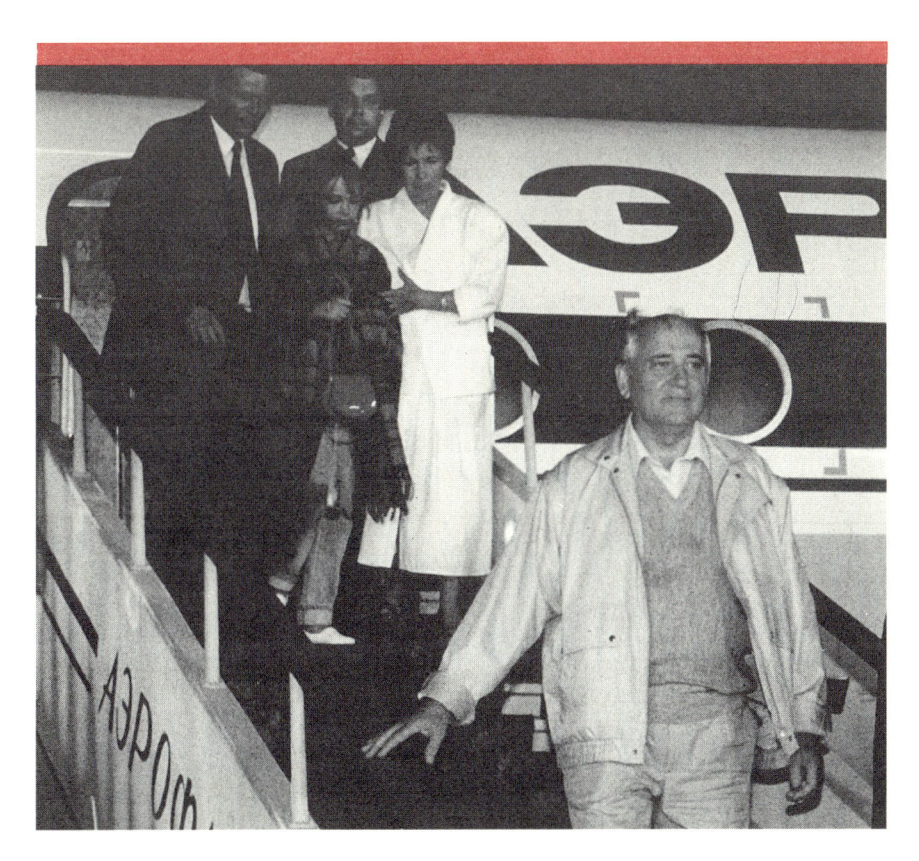

Gorbachev and his family return to Moscow after the failed coup.

Reporters crowded by the plane as wary security guards, then Gorbachev, and finally his family made their way down the stairs. There were reporters and cameras at the foot of the stairs, and Gorbachev paused before them briefly.

His aide, Yevgeny Primakov, tried to move Gorbachev past the reporters. "No, Mikhail Sergeyevich is tired," Primakov told the waiting reporters. "The car is waiting. We should go."

But for just a moment Gorbachev stood still. "No, wait," the Soviet president said softly. "I want to breathe the air of freedom in Moscow."[17]

chapter 10

New Flag over the Kremlin

In the aftermath of the failed coup, two pictures remained in people's minds. One was of Mikhail Gorbachev, just after his return to Moscow, making his way down the airplane stairs. Gorbachev looked tired and hesitant. He was not a defeated man, but he looked like a severely drained one. The other picture was of Boris Yeltsin addressing the people from atop a tank outside the Russian White House. Yeltsin looked bold, defiant, confident, and unafraid. To many the pictures were perfect symbols of the moment in history. Gorbachev belonged to the tired and weary past. It was Yeltsin's turn now to lead Russia into the future.

The defeat of the coup unleashed a massive wave of anger against the Communist Party throughout the Soviet Union. In both Moscow and St. Petersburg (the former Leningrad), thousands of Russian citizens took to the streets to denounce the Communist system. When Yuri Prokofiev, head of the Moscow party, tried to leave his office on August 22, he was seized by a huge crowd of Muscovites and immediately placed under arrest for his role in supporting the coup. An even larger crowd gathered outside the headquarters of the KGB, the old

Lubyanka prison on Dzerzhinsky Square. Soon the crowd was busy trying to bring down the mammoth statue of Felix Dzerzhinsky, the first head of the Soviet secret police. When Gavril Popov, the reformist mayor of Moscow, heard of his citizens' struggle, he immediately dispatched a team of city workers to remove the statue for them. The crowd cheered enthusiastically as city workers loaded Dzerzhinsky onto a large flatbed truck and carted him away to a nearby vacant lot. Soon the lot would be filled with toppled statues of former Soviet heroes—a kind of scrapheap of Communist icons.

Boris Yeltsin also realized that the time had come to deal the Communist Party a mortal blow. On August 21 he issued a decree closing down *Pravda* and five other Communist newspapers. He authorized Russian troops to seal off all local party headquarters on Russian territory and to confiscate files, records, and other evidence of Communist misdeeds. Apparently, party officials had worked feverishly in the days following the coup, destroying all evidence of past wrongdoings. There were reports that party workers had used secret tunnels and passageways out of the central headquarters to transport truckloads of damning material to the city dump. Others said that when the Soviet-made paper shredders inside party headquarters broke down due to overuse, leading party officials began tearing up files with their bare hands. Now, with Russian troops in control of the situation, there would be no further opportunities to destroy evidence.

Yeltsin had even bolder actions in mind. On the morning of August 23, he and Gorbachev appeared together before a special session of the Russian parliament. Gorbachev had barely begun speaking when he was interrupted by hecklers. One lawmaker in the audience demanded that Gorbachev explain why he had appointed men like Yanayev and Lukyanov in the first place. Other members of the parliament rose and demanded to know why Gorbachev insisted on defending the party in spite of the increasing evidence against it.

Yeltsin joined in the grilling of Gorbachev. When Gorbachev explained that he had not had a chance to read the minutes of the August 19 meeting at which the members of his own government agreed to launch the coup against him, Yeltsin rose from his seat and strode toward Gorbachev at the podium. He handed the Soviet president a sheaf of papers and said, "Read them!"

Gorbachev complied. Before a national television audience, Gorbachev perused the minutes and read how, one after another, men whom he had appointed had betrayed him. When, in a soft voice, he conceded, "This whole government has got to resign," the assembly erupted in a loud cheer.[1] It would be the only applause Gorbachev would receive that day.

Yeltsin pressed on. He continued to stand at Gorbachev's side, seeming almost to tower over him. "Boris Nikoayevich," Gorbachev pleaded meekly, "my situation right now is hard enough. Don't make it more difficult for me."[2] When Gorbachev insisted that any decision on nationalizing party property must be decided through the process of further negotiations on a new union treaty, Yeltsin interrupted him by theatrically waving a fountain pen in the air and asking the assembled parliament, "And now, on a lighter note, shall we now sign the decree suspending the activities of the Russian Communist Party?"

Gorbachev was flabbergasted. "What are you doing?"

he asked. "I haven't read this."

Before Gorbachev could say another word, Yeltsin announced, "The decree is hereby signed."[3] With a stroke of his pen, Boris Yeltsin had, in effect, signed the Bolshevik death warrant.

▼ ▲ ▼

The next day, August 24, Gorbachev joined Boris Yeltsin and tens of thousands of other Soviet citizens in a memorial service for Dmitri Komar, Ilya Krichevsky, and Vladimir Usov, the three men who had died as a result of the attempted coup. Yeltsin led the funeral procession down Kalinin Prospeckt and toward the Russian White House. When it reached Manezh Square, where the service was to take place, Gorbachev finally arrived. He looked grim and exhausted. His eyes welled with tears as

Boris Yeltsin attends a memorial service for three victims of the attempted coup.

he expressed his condolences to the parents of the three dead men and as he bent to lay flowers on their coffins. "I bow down before these young people," Gorbachev told the crowd. "They gave everything, even their lives."[4]

When he arrived back at his Kremlin office following the funeral, Gorbachev issued a statement announcing his resignation as general secretary of the Communist Party of the Soviet Union. Gorbachev then signed two decrees that some characterized as the "death blow to the party." As president, he ordered that all members of political parties immediately cease their activities within the government, armed forces, and KGB. The Communist Party had long derived its unrivalled power through the influence it exerted within the institutions of the state. Now Gorbachev had ended that influence and had cut back that power. Second, Gorbachev ordered the seizure of all Communist Party property. Now the national government—and the governments of the various republics—could lay claim to the Communists' vast holdings: office buildings, printing plants, special shops, hotels and resorts, as well as the homes and *dachas* of leading party officials. Overnight the party was bankrupt.

Gorbachev pressed on, throwing in his lot completely with Yeltsin and the other proponents of this "second Russian revolution." He ordered all the ministers in his cabinet to resign. A new governing council was created composed entirely of allies of reform.

Gorbachev believed that by sacrificing the party, the Soviet Union itself might be preserved. Yet his decrees seemed to have almost the opposite effect. Without the dictatorial force of the Communist Party holding it together, the USSR quickly splintered. One republic after another declared its independence from the central government.

The Russian Federation had already declared the sovereignty of its laws over those of the union. The three Baltic republics—Estonia, Latvia, and Lithuania—had already declared their independence, as had the republic of Georgia. On August 24 the Ukrainian parliament voted to secede. Within a week the parliaments of six more republics would do the same: Byelorussia on August 25, Moldavia on August 27, Azerbaijan on August 28, Uzbekistan and Kirgizstan on August 31. Declarations of independence would be passed by Tadzhikistan and Armenia during September 1991. "There can be no illusion: the Soviet Union no longer exists," exulted one advocate of Ukrainian independence.[5]

▼ ▲ ▼

But few were willing to state with confidence what the next stage might be. Many, including both Gorbachev and Yeltsin, feared that the rapid disintegration of the USSR might unleash bitter rivalries among the different republics. There was danger of civil war breaking out within several republics as well.

In the Georgian capital, Tbilisi, thousands had taken to the streets to protest the increasingly authoritarian rule of the republic's new president, Zviad Gamsakhurdia. Many feared that widespread violence might erupt in Georgia when the restraining influence of Soviet troops was removed.

Similar fears existed in Moldavia, where a very complicated political situation saw four competing groups vying for power. While some Moldavians favored the continuation of the republic's relationship with Moscow, most Moldavians were in favor of some form of independence.

But the pro-independence forces were divided among themselves, with one party favoring complete independence and another wanting eventual reunification with Romania. Another opposition group, the Gaugauz, demanded sovereignty for those areas of Moldavia inhabited by the republic's Turkish minority.

Leaders in several republics were growing increasingly fearful of Yeltsin's ambitions as head of the mammoth Russian Federation. The leaders of the other republics bristled when Yeltsin insisted that Russians be named to both the presidency and the vice presidency of any new union. "We will never be anyone's little brother," declared Kazakhstan's Nazarbayev,[6] and he warned that inordinate Russian influence might give rise to open warfare among the various republics.

Gorbachev eventually managed to assemble representatives of eleven republics (all except the Baltics and Moldavia) and reopen negotiations at Novo-Ogaryovo. Under the terms of a preliminary agreement reached by ten of the eleven—the Georgian representative abstained from voting—a new Union of Sovereign States was to be established. On September 5, the Congress of People's Deputies voted to approve the preliminary agreement.

However, within a few weeks the process of drafting a new union treaty was in deep trouble. By the end of the fall, Armenia had joined the other Caucasus republics, Georgia and Moldavia, in abandoning the negotiations. Likewise in November, Gorbachev announced that President Ayaz Mutabilov of Azerbaijan would no longer be coming to Novo-Ogaryovo "because of the difficult situation in his republic."[7]

The biggest blow against the formation of the Union of Sovereign States, however, was dealt by the leaders of the

Ukraine. With a population of more than 60 million, the Ukraine was the second largest of the Soviet republics. It also contained vast resources, much of the country's heavy industry, and its most fertile farmland. In November 1991, President Leonid Kravchuk of the Ukraine announced that he would not attend the next meeting at Novo-Ogaryovo.

Gorbachev decided that desperate measures were needed to salvage the union treaty. To force the hands of the leaders of the republics, he announced on November 25 that he and the republican leaders would, that very day, initial a completed draft of the treaty. Gorbachev's announcement came as a surprise to everyone—especially the leaders of the republics themselves! There was, in fact, no draft treaty. Gorbachev's ploy backfired badly. When Gorbachev tried to force his proposals for a final draft on the other leaders, they unanimously rejected it. Once again, Gorbachev stormed out of the room. Describing events later, Boris Yeltsin wrote the following.

We were left alone in the room, and precisely then, as a heavy, oppressive silence hung over the room, we suddenly realized that it was over. We were meeting here for the last time. The Novo-Ogaryovo saga had drawn to a close. There would be no more progress in that direction, and never would be. We would have to seek and conceive of something new.[8]

▼ ▲ ▼

On December 1 the people of the Ukraine voted overwhelmingly in favor of complete independence. One week later, on the evening of December 7, Yeltsin, Ukrainian president Kravchuk, and Byelorussian leader Stanislav Shushkevich traveled to Minsk, the capital of the Byelorussian Republic. From there, they made their way out of the city to a hunting lodge deep inside a government nature reserve. Working into the early hours of the next morning, the three leaders and their assistants drafted a treaty establishing a new government to replace the USSR.

The next day, Yeltsin, Kravchuk, and Shushkevich traveled back to Minsk. At a joint press conference, they announced that they had agreed to form a new confederation, the Commonwealth of Independent States (CIS). The other Soviet republics would be invited to join the CIS as well, the three leaders concluded.

The world was stunned by the sudden announcement. Most shocked of all, perhaps, was Gorbachev. "This agreement has its positive moments," Gorbachev began, struggling to put the best face possible on his deteriorating situation. But, he continued, "the speed at which the document appeared is baffling."[9] The leaders of three republics had decided on their own to disband the Soviet Union. The agreement had not been discussed by the legislatures—or citizens—of the three republics involved, let alone those of the other nine republics that now constituted the USSR. Furthermore, Gorbachev added, negotiations were already in progress on the formation of the Union of Sovereign States. That issue should be dealt with before any new proposals were put forward.

Many feared that a great power struggle between Yeltsin and Gorbachev was now at hand. The most troubling concern was the question of who would control the Soviet Union's vast military resources—especially its nuclear weapons. Robert Gates, director of the CIA, warned that the Soviet Union could become "dangerously unstable" should a power struggle between Moscow and the republics break out.[10]

Soon, however, it became obvious that the political momentum now lay with Yeltsin and the other proponents of the CIS. On December 13, the leaders of five central Asia republics—Kazakhstan, Kirgizstan, Tadzhikistan, Turkmenistan, and Uzbekistan—announced that they too had agreed to join the new commonwealth. Gorbachev realized that his days in power were drawing to a close. The Soviet Union must be allowed to die a peaceful death, with no further threats of bloodshed, violence, or civil strife.

On December 17, Yeltsin and Gorbachev met at the Kremlin to work out the final details of the transfer of

Yeltsin and Shushkevich at the announcement of the formation of the Commonwealth of Independent States

power. They agreed that as of midnight on December 31, 1991, the USSR would cease to exist. Gorbachev would officially resign as president six days before, on the evening of December 25.

On that night, Mikhail Gorbachev addressed the people of the Soviet Union for the last time as their leader. He began by recounting the situation in the country when he had taken over, more than six years before.

> *Fate had it that when I found myself at the head of the state, it was already clear that all was not well in the land. We have plenty of everything: land, oil and gas, other natural riches, and God gave us lots of intelligence and talent. Yet we lived much worse than developed countries, and kept falling farther and farther behind.*

The country was suffocating under the heavily centralized Communist system, Gorbachev continued. "Everything had to be changed radically." But the process of restructuring the country turned out to be much more complicated than anyone had anticipated. Still, there had been important accomplishments. "This society has acquired freedom," Gorbachev said. It had "liberated itself politically and spiritually." But now the time had come for him to resign.

> *I am leaving my post with apprehension, but also with hope, with faith in you, your wisdom and force of spirit. We are the heirs to a great civilization; and its rebirth into a new, modern, and dignified life now depends on one and all.*[11]

The next morning, Gorbachev rode to the Kremlin as he had so many previous mornings. He had resigned, but there was still last-minute business to transact in the closing days of the USSR. But when Gorbachev arrived at his office deep in the labyrinthlike corridors of the Kremlin, he saw that a different nameplate was on the door: a brand-new one, its gold lettering shining brightly and forming the name YELTSIN, B. N. Yeltsin, Gorbachev's old rival—his sometime opponent, sometime ally—was already inside at his desk, busily at work.

Overnight, representatives of the Russian government had moved their offices out of the Russian parliament building and had assumed control of the Kremlin. Likewise, control of the Soviet military forces, including the top secret nuclear codes, had been transferred to Yeltsin. Immediately following Gorbachev's speech, the flag of the Soviet Union had been lowered from its pole high above Red Square.

Gone at last was the red banner of Communism, with its gold hammer and sickle emblem, that had flown over Moscow since 1917. Gone was the flag that had flown over revolution, famine, terror, and war—times of hope and despair and confusion.

Then, the next day, as an eager crowd below watched and cheered, a new flag rose slowly on the pole. A new day had arrived, and there was now a new flag flying over the Kremlin. A new, different banner, bearing three stripes—red, white, and blue. And yet this flag, like the country over which it flew, was not entirely new. Russia's flag had had the same design in the days of the czar, in the years before the Bolsheviks had come to power. The flag that had flown over Russia's tumultuous past would now fly over Russia's uncertain future.

The Russian flag flies over the Kremlin.

Postscript

In the years following the collapse of the Soviet government, conflict and uncertainty continued to characterize the situation in the former Soviet republics. The Commonwealth of Independent States failed to develop as a viable successor to the USSR. Instead, the various republics all went their own ways, with only minimal relationship to one another.

In the largest republic, Russia, the situation grew extremely complicated. While President Boris Yeltsin's hold on power was strengthened by the resignation of Soviet leader Mikhail Gorbachev, there soon arose bitter and intense rivalries within the government of the Russian Federation. In March 1993, Yeltsin's opponents attempted to impeach him and remove him from office. Yeltsin narrowly survived the impeachment attempt. But the struggle for power within Russia grew so intense that in the fall of 1993, Yeltsin dissolved the Russian parliament and ordered new elections. Opposition legislators defied the president's orders and barricaded themselves inside the Russian White House, where Yeltsin had bravely stood up against the hardline coup of August 1991. Yeltsin then moved with massive force against his opponents: He ordered the Russian army to launch a fullscale siege of the parliament building. Heavy artillery bombarded the building, causing heavy damage—and the deaths of 140 supporters of the opposition. Finally, the opposition was forced to surrender, but Yeltsin's ruthlessness was widely criticized, both within Russia and in the West.

In Chechnya, a new government had declared its independence from Moscow in 1991. The Russian government, however, refused to recognize Chechnya's sovereignty. In December 1994, a massive Russian force invaded Chechnya, believing it could score a quick and easy victory. Instead, the conflict turned into a long and costly stalemate, which would eventually claim the lives of thousands and engender even greater hostility against Yeltsin and his government.

Meanwhile, reformers within Russia questioned Yeltsin's dedication to democratic ideals and urged him to make even more far-reaching reforms. Russian nationalists criticized him for his conciliatory attitude toward the West and the loss of Russian control of the former Soviet republics. The newly reorganized Communist Party, led by Gennady Zyuganov, gained increasing support from many Russians as they struggled to make ends meet amidst rising prices and economic uncertainty. Widescale rumors about the poor state of Yeltsin's health weakened the president's position further.

In elections in December 1995, the Communists gained control of the lower house of the Russian legislature, and Zyuganov seemed poised to unseat Yeltsin. However, as the presidential campaign progressed, many Russians seemed increasingly concerned about the possibility of the restoration of the Communist Party to power. On July 3, 1996, the final round of the Russian presidential election was held, and Yeltsin scored a clear victory over Zyuganov.

Chapter Notes

Chapter 1
1. Mikhail Heller and Aleksandr Nekrich, *Utopia in Power: The History of the Soviet Union from 1917 to the Present* (New York: Summit Books, 1986), 33.
2. Leonard Schapiro. *The Communist Party of the Soviet Union* (New York: Random House, 1960), 167.
3. Heller and Nekrich, *Utopia in Power*, 52
4. *Ibid.*, 47
5. *Ibid.*, 66
6. Roy A. Medvedev, *Let History Judge: The Origins and Consequences of Stalinism* (New York: Popular Library, 1973), 24.
7. *Ibid.*, 25

Chapter 2
1. Marx-Engels-Lenin Institute, *Joseph Stalin: A Political Biography* (New York: International Publishers, 1949), 50.
2. Michael Kort, *The Soviet Colossus: A History of the USSR* (Boston: Unwin Hyman, 1990), 171.
3. *Ibid.*, 173.
4. Heller and Nekrich, *Utopia in Power*, 250.
5. Kort, *The Soviet Colossus*, 190–1.
6. Joseph Stalin, *The Great Patriotic War of the Soviet Union* (New York: International Publishers, 1945), 9.

Chapter 3
1. Nikita Khrushchev, "Premier Nikita Khrushchev, in a 'Secret Speech,' Tears Down Stalin's Reputation," in *Lend Me Your Ears: Great Speeches in History*, ed. by William Safire (New York: W. W. Norton, 1992), 807.

2. *Ibid.*, 809–10.
3. Nicholas V. Riasanovsky, *A History of Russia*, 2nd ed. (New York: Oxford University Press, 1969), 601.

Chapter 4
1. Heller and Nekrich, *Utopia in Power*, 643.
2. John Dornberg, *The New Tsars: Russia Under Stalin's Heirs* (Garden City, NY: Doubleday & Co., 1972), 317–8.
3. Hedrick Smith, *The New Russians* (New York: Avon Books, 1991), 24.

Chapter 5
1. Robert G. Kaiser, *Why Gorbachev Happened: His Triumphs, His Failure, and His Fall* (New York: Simon & Schuster, 1992), 84.
2. *Ibid.*, 98.
3. *Ibid.*, 119.
4. *Ibid.*, 127.
5. *Ibid.*, 126–7.

Chapter 6
1. Gail Sheehy, *The Man Who Changed the World: The Lives of Mikhail S. Gorbachev* (New York: HarperCollins, 1990), 240.
2. Steven Otfinosky, *Mikhail Gorbachev: The Soviet Innovator* (New York: Fawcett Columbine, 1989), 85.
3. Andrei Sakharov, *Memoirs* (New York: Alfred A. Knopf, 1990), 615.
4. Mikhail Gorbachev, *Perestroika: New Thinking for Our Country and the World* (New York: Harper & Row, 1987), xiv.
5. *Ibid.*, 3.
6. Boris Yeltsin, *Against the Grain: An Autobiography* (New York: Summit Books, 1990), 191.
7. Kaiser, *Why Gorbachev Happened*, 181–2.
8. Yeltsin, *Against the Grain*, 199.
9. Kaiser, *Why Gorbachev Happened*, 189.
10. Smith, *The New Russians*, 443.

Chapter 7

1. Dusko Doder and Louise Branson, *Gorbachev: Heretic in the Kremlin* (New York: Penguin Books, 1991), 404.
2. Smith, *The New Russians*, 510.
3. *Ibid.*, 509.
4. Kaiser, *Why Gorbachev Happened*, 320.
5. *Ibid.*, 321.
6. *Ibid.*, 331.

Chapter 8

1. Kaiser, *Why Gorbachev Happened*, 336.
2. *Ibid.*, 349.
3. *Ibid.*, 379.
4. *Ibid.*, 382.
5. *The New York Times*, December 27, 1990, 1.
6. Kaiser, *Why Gorbachev Happened*, 392.
7. *Ibid.*, 394.
8. *Ibid.*, 395.
9. Mikhail Gorbachev, *The August Coup: The Truth and the Lessons* (New York: HarperCollins, 1991), 13.
10. Kaiser, *Why Gorbachev Happened*, 403.
11. *Ibid.*, 409.
12. *Ibid.*, 410.
13. *Ibid.*, 411.
14. *Ibid.*, 416.
15. *Ibid.*, 417.
16. *Ibid.*, 421.

Chapter 9

1. Gorbachev, *The August Coup*, 18-9.
2. *Ibid.*, 19.
3. *Ibid.*, 20–1.
4. *Ibid.*, 21–3.
5. David Remnick, *Lenin's Tomb: The Last Days of the Soviet Empire* (New York: Vintage Books, 1994), 457.
6. *The New York Times*, August 19, 1991, 1.

Chapter Notes   149

7. Boris Yeltsin, *The Struggle for Russia* (New York: Times Books, 1994), 54.
8. Remnick, *Lenin's Tomb*, 466.
9. Gurbachev, *The August Coup*, 27.
10. Remnick, *Lenin's Tomb*, 483.
11. *Ibid.*, 483.
12. *Ibid.*, 484.
13. *Ibid.*, 484.
14. Smith, *The New Russians*, 645.
15. *Ibid.*, 645.
16. Remnick, *Lenin's Tomb*, 488.
17. Smith, *The New Russians*, 646.

Chapter 10
1. *The New York Times*, August 24, 1991, 6.
2. Smith, *The New Russians*, 654.
3. *The New York Times*, August 24, 1991, 7.
4. *The New York Times*, August 25, 1991, 15.
5. *The New York Times*, August 27, 1991, 1.
6. Smith, *The New Russians*, 656.
7. Yeltsin, *The Struggle for Russia*, 110.
8. *Ibid.*, 110.
9. *The New York Times*, December 10, 1991, 18.
10. *The New York Times*, December 11, 1991, 18.
11. *The New York Times*, December 26, 1991, 12.

Glossary

Allies—France, Great Britain, the Soviet Union, the United States, and the nations that sided with them against the Axis forces (Germany, Italy, Japan, and their supporters) during World War II.

capitalism—An economic system in which property is owned by private individuals or groups and the free-market forces of supply and demand operate.

coalition—A group composed of members of two or more political parties who have joined forces to achieve common objectives.

Communism—An economic and political system in which all property is owned by the state and the society is placed under the control of a single (Communist) party.

conservative—An individual who is slow to embrace political and social change.

dissident—An individual who speaks out in opposition to those in power. The term generally refers to those who oppose their nation's Communist government.

dogmatist—An individual who believes that the doctrines of a particular philosophy must be applied strictly.

fascist—Referring to a political system characterized by a strong, authoritarian central government and in which the rights of opposition parties and individuals are severely limited.

liberalism—Belief in the desirability of change or reform in a system or institution.

nationalism—Strong feelings for the interests of one's own national group or country; the desire for national independence.

parliamentary democracy—A political system in which voters elect representatives to a legislature (or parliament). The legislators in turn decide who will be the leader of the government.

revisionism—A form of Communism under which political leaders apply political doctrines according to the changing conditions in a particular nation.

socialism—An economic and social philosophy in which all property is owned commonly for the good of the whole society.

Stalinism—A strict form of Communism, under which the rule of the Communist leadership is tightly maintained and opposing viewpoints are severely repressed.

Time Line

1917 (March) Czar Nicholas II is overthrown and a provisional government headed by Prince Lvov assumes control of Russia. (July) Alexander Kerensky replaces Prince Lvov as head of the provisional government. (November) The Bolshevik party, headed by Lenin, seizes power and establishes Soviet Russia, the world's first Communist state.

1918–1920 Civil war rages throughout Russia, as the White army attempts unsuccessfully to topple the Soviet regime.

1922 Union of Soviet Socialist Republics is established.

1924 Death of Lenin. Stalin and Trotsky struggle for power.

1929 Stalin's dictatorship over the party becomes secure. First Five-Year Plan begins.

1929–1933 The collectivization of the Soviet Union's farmland costs the lives of millions.

1934 Sergei Kirov, first secretary of the Leningrad Communist Party, is assassinated. In response, hundreds of thousands are arrested. By 1938, a mass terror campaign will have claimed the lives of millions of Soviet citizens. Millions of others are sent to concentration camps.

1939 The USSR signs a nonagression pact with Nazi Germany. As part of this agreement, the Soviet Union seizes control of Moldavia and the Baltic republics (Estonia, Latvia, and Lithuania).

1941 Germany invades the Soviet Union, forcing the USSR to enter World War II.

1945 Nazi Germany is defeated and driven from Soviet soil. Following the war the nations of Eastern Europe come under the control of Communist governments.

1953	Death of Stalin. Within little more than a year, Nikita Khrushchev assumes full control over the Soviet party and government.
1956	In a secret speech at a Communist Party congress, Khrushchev denounces the crimes of Stalin. A campaign of de-Stalinization is launched throughout Soviet society.
1961–1963	The rivalry of the USSR and Communist China splits the world Communist movement.
1964	Khrushchev is removed from power.
1965–1982	Leonid Brezhnev holds full control over the USSR. Brezhnev's years in office will later be referred to as the Era of Stagnation.
1982	Yuri Andropov replaces Brezhnev as Soviet leader and promises to crack down on corruption and impose "discipline" on Soviet society.
1984	Andropov dies and is replaced by Konstantin Chernenko.
1985	Death of Chernenko. Mikhail Gorbachev is selected as general secretary of the Soviet Communist Party.
1986	(February) Gorbachev calls for *glasnost*—openness—in admitting past Soviet mistakes and facing current problems. Later Gorbachev speeds up the pace of reform and calls for *perestroika or* restructuring.
1987–1988	Perestroika sweeps the Soviet Union, bringing about increased political freedom but little improvement in the quality of life. Within the Communist Party, the rift between hard-liners and reformers widens.
1989	(March) Elections are held for delegates to a new Congress of People's Deputies. Over 400 radical reformers, gain seats in the new congress.

(May) The Congress of People's Deputies begins to meet in Moscow.

(Fall–Winter) Political unrest leads to the fall of Communist governments throughout Eastern Europe. |

154 The Soviet Turmoil

1990 (February) The Congress of People's Deputies removes the leading role of the Communist Party from the Soviet constitution. The powers of the presidency of the USSR are greatly increased, and Gorbachev is elected to the post.

(March) Lithuania declares its independence, a move not recognized by the central government in Moscow.

(May) Boris Yeltsin is elected president of Russia.

(Summer) A majority of Soviet republics declare their sovereignty or independence.

Discontent against Gorbachev's government continues to mount.

1991 (January) The Soviet government seeks to crack down on the independence movement in neighboring the Baltic countries.

(March) Gorbachev names a new Security Council comprised largely of antidemocratic hard-liners. Boris Yeltsin calls for open opposition to the Soviet leadership.

(April) Gorbachev and the leaders of nine of the USSR's fifteen republics enter into negotiations for a new union treaty.

(August) Hard-liners within the Soviet government attempt to remove Gorbachev from power. Within four days the coup falls apart and Gorbachev returns to Moscow. Yeltsin moves to crush the power of the Communist Party within the Russian republic. As the party collapses, Gorbachev resigns as general secretary.

(August–September) As one after another all 15 republics declare their independence from the USSR, Gorbachev desperately seeks to negotiate a new union treaty to no avail.

(December 8) The presidents of Russia, Ukraine, and Byelorussia agree to dissolve the Soviet Union and form a new Commonwealth of Independent States (CIS).

(December 31) The Union of Soviet Socialist Republics ceases to exist.

Selected Bibliography

Adams, Arthur E. *Stalin and His Times*. New York: Holt, Rinehart and Winston, 1972.

Beschloss, Michael R. *The Crisis Years: Kennedy and Khrushchev, 1960–1963*. New York: HarperCollins, Edward Burlingame Books, 1991.

Brown, Archie, and Michael Kaser, eds. *The Soviet Union Since the Fall of Khrushchev*. New York: The Free Press, 1975.

Conquest, Robert. *The Harvest of Sorrow: Soviet Collectivization and the Terror-Famine*. New York: Oxford University Press, 1986.

Crankshaw, Edward. *Khrushchev: A Career*. New York: Viking Press, 1966.

d'Encausse, Helene Carriere. *The End of the Soviet Empire: The Triumph of the Nations*. New York: Basic Books, 1993.

Doder, Dusko, and Louise Branson. *Gorbachev: Heretic in the Kremlin*. New York: Penguin Books, 1991.

Dornberg, John. *The New Tsars: Russia Under Stalin's Heirs*. Garden City, NY: Doubleday & Co., 1972.

Felshman, Neil. *Gorbachev, Yeltsin, and the Last Days of the Soviet Empire*. New York: St. Martin's Press, 1992.

Goldman, Marshall I. *What Went Wrong with Perestroika?* New York: W. W. Norton, 1991.

Gorbachev, Mikhail. *The August Coup: The Truth and the Lessons.* New York: HarperCollins, 1991.

Gorbachev, Mikhail. *Perestroika: New Thinking for Our Country and the World.* New York: Harper & Row, 1987.

Gwertzman, Bernard, and Michael T. Kaufman, eds. *The Collapse of Communism.* New York: Times Books, 1990.

Halle, Louis J. *The Cold War as History.* New York: Harper & Row, 1967.

Heller, Mikhail, and Aleksandr Nekrich, eds. *Utopia in Power: The History of the Soviet Union from 1917 to the Present.* New York: Summit Books, 1986.

Kaiser, Robert G. *Why Gorbachev Happened: His Triumphs, His Failure, and His Fall.* New York: Simon & Schuster, 1992.

Kennan, George E. *Russia and the West Under Lenin and Stalin.* Boston: Little, Brown & Company, 1961.

Khrushchev, Nikita S. *Khrushchev Remembers.* Boston: Little, Brown & Company, 1970.

Kort, Michael. *The Soviet Colossus: A History of the USSR.* Boston: Unwin Hyman, 1990.

Medvedev, Roy A. *Let History Judge: The Origins and Consequences of Stalinism.* New York: Vintage Books, 1973.

Nove, Alec. *An Economic History of the USSR: 1917–1991.* London: Penguin Books, 1992.

Remnick, David. *Lenin's Tomb: The Last Days of the Soviet Empire*. New York: Vintage Books, 1994.

Riasanovsky, Nicholas V. *A History of Russia*. Second edition. New York: Oxford University Press, 1969.

Sakharov, Andrei. *Memoirs*. New York: Alfred A. Knopf, 1990.

Schapiro, Leonard. *The Communist Party of the Soviet Union*. New York: Random House, 1960.

Sheehy, Gail. *The Man Who Changed the World: The Lives of Mikhail Gorbachev*. New York: HarperCollins, 1990.

Shipler, David K. *Russia: Broken Idols, Solemn Dreams*. New York: Penguin Books, 1984.

Smith, Hedrick. *The New Russians*. New York: Avon Books, 1991.

Tismaneanu, Vladimir. *Reinventing Politics: Eastern Europe from Stalin to Havel*. New York: The Free Press, 1992.

von Raugh, Georg. *A History of Soviet Russia*. Sixth edition. New York: Praeger Publishers, 1972.

Yeltsin, Boris. *Against the Grain: An Autobiography*. New York: Summit Books, 1990.

Yeltsin, Boris. *The Struggle for Russia*. New York: Times Books, 1994.

Index

Abuladze, Tengiz 69
Achalov, Vladislav 126
Afghanistan 55, 64, 126
Ageyev, Genii 119
Akmatova, Anna 73
Albania 30
alcohol abuse 51, 54, 62–64
Alexandra (czarina) 7, 16
Alpha Group 121, 126–127
Andreyava, Nina 77–78
Andropov, Yuri 38–39, 53–55, 56, 58, 62
April Theses 10
Armenia 82, 92, 104, 137, 138
arms limitations talks 64–66, 70–71
Article Six 88–90
Azerbaijan 82, 92, 137, 139

Bakatin, Vadim 101
Baklanov, Oleg 116, 119
Beria, Lavrenti 26, 33–34, 36
Berlin Wall 41–42, 87
Boldin, Valeri 116, 119
Bolsheviks 9, 11–16, 135
Bonner, Elena 88
Brakov, Yevgeny 79–80
Brezhnev, Galina 54
Brezhnev, Leonid 44–50, 53, 55, 77
Brezhnev Doctrine 48
Bukharin, Nikolai 21, 25, 26
Bulganin, Nikolai 34, 40
Bulgaria 30, 87
Burbulis, Gennadi 128
Bush, George 114
Byelorussia 14, 61, 66, 91, 137, 140

Castro, Fidel 42
Ceaușescu, Nicolae 87, 95
Cheka 16–17

Chernenko, Constantin 53–54, 56–57, 62
Chernobyl 66–69
China 40–41, 82
collectivization 22–24, 49
Commonwealth of Independent States (CIS) 140, 142
concentration camps 17, 23, 24
Congress of People's Deputies 79, 83–85, 87–88, 92, 102, 108
corruption 51, 54, 56, 62
Cuban missile crisis 42, 55
Czechoslovakia 30, 47–48, 87

Daniel, Yuli 47
democratization 79, 107
demonstrations 37, 94–95, 108, 109, 122–124, 125–126, 137
dissidents 52, 55
Doctors' Plot 31–32, 36
Dubček, Alexander 47–48
Dzerzhinsky, Felix 16, 133

East Germany 30, 41, 87
economy 21, 34, 42, 48–51, 59, 66, 82–83, 89–90, 95–96, 98–101
elections 79–81, 85, 91, 112
Estonia 14, 27, 81, 85–86, 91, 104, 107, 108, 137

February Revolution. *See* March Revolution
films 69–70
Finland 14, 112
five-year plans 21–24, 49

Gamsakhurdia, Zviad 137
Gates, Robert 141
Geneva, summit conference 64–66
Georgia 62, 69, 82, 92, 104, 108, 137, 138

Index

GKchP (State Committee for the State of Emergency) 118, 119, 120, 122, 127, 128
glasnost 66, 68, 69, 72, 77, 78
Gorbachev, Mikhail 56–57, 58–79, 82–84, 87–96, 97–119, 124–125, 129–132, 133–143
Gorbachev, Raisa 61, 84, 116, 129, 130
Gosplan 50
Grachev, Pavel 118, 126, 127
Grishin, Viktor 57, 58
Gromov, Boris 101, 114
Gromyko, Andrei 58–59, 61
Gulag Archipelago, The 52

hard-liners 74, 77, 88, 103, 107, 108–109, 118, 119, 125, 126, 128, 129
Hitler, Adolf 27, 28–30
Hungary 30, 37–39, 87

Inter-Regional Group 81, 92, 94
Isvestia 95
Ivashko, Vladimir 129

Jews 31–32, 55, 74

Kamenev, Lev 20–21, 25
Kaplan, Dora 17
Kazakhstan 61, 138, 142
Kazannik, Aleksei 85
Kennedy, John F. 42
Kerensky, Aleksandr 11–13
KGB 40, 52, 53, 71, 93, 101, 113, 116, 126, 127, 132–133, 136
Khasbulatov, Ruslan 121, 122
Khrushchev, Nikita 33–43, 45, 46, 53
Kirgizstan 137, 142
Kirov, Sergei 24–25
Kobets, Konstantin 123
Kornilov, Lavr 12
Kosygin, Aleksei 44–45
Kravchuk, Leonid 139, 140
Kryuchkov, Vladimir 101–102, 107, 108, 113, 118–119, 120, 126, 127–128, 129–130

Landsbergis, Vytautas 92
Latvia 14, 27, 66, 81, 85–86, 91, 104, 107, 108, 137
Lebed (general) 126, 127
Lenin, Vladimir Ilyich 9–12, 14, 15–18, 19–20, 40
Lenin's Testament 17–18
Ligachev, Yegor 74–75, 77–78, 97–98, 103
Lithuania 14, 27, 51, 66, 81, 85–86, 91, 92–93, 104–107, 108, 137
Lukyanov, Anatoly 119, 129, 130
Lvov, Georgi 8

Malenkov, Georgi 33, 34
Mao Zedong 40
March Revolution 7–9
Medvedev, Roy 80
Memorial Society 74
Mensheviks 9, 15
Moldavia 27, 81, 82, 104, 137, 138
Molotov, V.M. 27, 33
Mutabilov, Ayaz 139

Nagy, Imre 37–39
Nazarbayev, Nursyltan 120, 138
Nicholas II, czar 7–8, 16
Nine Plus One talks 109–110, 112, 113
nomenklatura 46
November Revolution 7, 13–14

October Revolution. *See* November Revolution
One Day in the Life of Ivan Denisovitch 46
Operation Thunder 126
Orwell, George 72

Pamyat 74
Pasternak, Boris 73
Pavlov, Valentin 112–113, 119, 128
perestroika 61, 68, 73, 74, 76, 77, 78, 83, 101, 103
Perestroika: New Thinking for Our Country and the World 73

Plekhanov, Yuri 116, 117, 119
Poland 14, 27, 30, 37, 87, 112
Popov, Gavril 94, 133
Prague Spring 47
Pravda 21, 46, 133
Primakov, Yevgeny 131
Prokofiev, Yri 132
Prunskiene, Kazimiera 104
Pugo, Boris 101, 105, 107, 108, 113, 119, 128

Rasputin, Grigori 7
Reagan, Ronald 64–66, 70
Red Army 15, 22, 26, 28–30
reformers 74, 80, 88, 103
Repentance 69–70
Reykjavík, summit conference 70–71
Ribbentrop, Joachim von 27
Romania 27, 30, 138
Russian Federation 97, 98, 100, 111, 137, 138
Rutskoi, Alexander 122, 129, 130
Rybakov, Anatoli 73
Ryzhkov, Nikolai 62, 95–96, 99, 112

Sajudis 91, 92–93
Sakharov, Andrei 52, 55, 71–72, 79–80, 87–89, 94
Salayev, Anatoly 127
secret police 16, 22, 23, 25, 31. *See also* Cheka, KGB
Serov, Ivan 40
Shatalin, Stanislav 98, 99, 100
Shenin, Oleg 116, 119
Shevardnadze, Eduard 62, 69, 75, 102–103, 104
show trials 25–26, 47
Shushkevich, Stanislav 140
Silayev, Ivan 129
Sinyavski, Andrei 47
Sobchak, Anatoly 124
Solzhenitsyn, Aleksandr 46, 52
Stalin, Josef 18, 19–32, 36–37, 40, 45, 53, 69, 73, 74, 77, 80
Suslov, Mikhail 43

Tadzhikistan 137, 142
Treaty of Brest-Litovsk 14–15
Trotsky, Leon 12–13, 15, 17, 18, 19–21, 25, 52
Turkmenistan 142

Ukraine 14, 23, 35, 61, 66, 81, 83, 91, 100, 104, 137, 139, 140
Union of Sovereign States 138, 139, 140
Uritsky, Mikhail 17
Uzbekistan 137, 142

Varennikov, Valentin 114, 117
Vyshinsky, Andrei 25

Warsaw Pact 38, 48
White Army 15
White House 121, 122, 125, 126, 127
World War I 7, 14–15

Yagdoa, Genrikh 26
Yakovlev, Aleksandr 62, 75, 78
Yanayev, Gennadi 103–104, 107, 108, 115, 117, 119–120, 125, 127
Yazov, Dmitri 101, 113, 119, 126, 128, 129, 130
Yeliseyev, A. S. 76
Yeltsin, Boris 62, 74–77, 79–80, 84–85, 90–91, 97–101, 107–108, 111–112, 113, 120–123, 125, 126, 128–130, 132–137, 139–143
Yevtushenko, Yevgeny 80
Yezhov, Nikolai 26
Yugoslavia 30, 77

Zaikov, Lev 60, 62
Zhirinovsky, Vladimir 112
Zhukov, Georgi 28, 39
Zinoviev, Grigori 20–21, 25